THE
EVERYTHING®
INVESTING IN YOUR 20s & 30s BOOK

Dear Reader,

The financial markets are more dangerous than ever. You should only invest through them if you are prepared and have the right knowledge. It is even more dangerous to trade them. But it can be done, and it can be done properly if you have good knowledge, have patience, and develop a plan. Those who don't prepare will almost certainly lose a lot of money and suffer a great deal of financial hardship.

This book has been written with the goal of helping young people invest their money wisely for the long haul. Its purpose is to help you understand how to get started, how to evaluate investments, how to make, buy, and sell decisions, and more importantly, when it's a good time to sell. I've done my best to make it as easy to read as possible and to give you good, sound information that will allow you to build upon your knowledge as you progress. Good luck!

Dr. Joe Duarte

Welcome to the EVERYTHING® Series!

These handy, accessible books give you all you need to tackle a difficult project, gain a new hobby, comprehend a fascinating topic, prepare for an exam, or even brush up on something you learned back in school but have since forgotten.

You can choose to read an Everything® book from cover to cover or just pick out the information you want from our four useful boxes: e-questions, e-facts, e-alerts, and e-ssentials.

We give you everything you need to know on the subject, but throw in a lot of fun stuff along the way, too.

We now have more than 400 Everything® books in print, spanning such wide-ranging categories as weddings, pregnancy, cooking, music instruction, foreign language, crafts, pets, New Age, and so much more. When you're done reading them all, you can finally say you know Everything®!

QUESTION

Answers to
common questions

FACT

Important snippets
of information

ALERT

Urgent
warnings

ESSENTIAL

Quick
handy tips

PUBLISHER Karen Cooper

MANAGING EDITOR, EVERYTHING® SERIES Lisa Laing

COPY CHIEF Casey Ebert

ASSISTANT PRODUCTION EDITOR Alex Guarco

ACQUISITIONS EDITOR Hillary Thompson

ASSOCIATE DEVELOPMENT EDITOR Eileen Mullan

EVERYTHING® SERIES COVER DESIGNER Erin Alexander

Visit the entire Everything® series at *www.everything.com*

THE
EVERYTHING®
INVESTING IN YOUR 20s & 30s BOOK

Learn how to manage your money and start investing for your future—now!

Joe Duarte, MD

Avon, Massachusetts

To readers, thinkers, and doers—young and old.

Published by Adams Media, a division of F+W Media, Inc.
57 Littlefield Street, Avon, MA 02322. U.S.A.
www.adamsmedia.com

Contains material adapted and abridged from *The Everything® Investing Book, 3rd Edition* by Michele Cagan, copyright © 2009 by F+W Media, Inc., ISBN 10: 1-59869-829-X, ISBN 13: 978-1-59869-829-9; and *The Everything® Personal Finance in Your 20s & 30s Book, 3rd Edition* by Howard Davidoff, copyright © 2012 by F+W Media, Inc., ISBN 10: 1-4405-4256-2, ISBN 13: 978-1-4405-4256-5.

ISBN 10: 1-4405-8085-5
ISBN 13: 978-1-4405-8085-7
eISBN 10: 1-4405-8086-3
eISBN 13: 978-1-4405-8086-4

Printed in the United States of America.

10   9   8   7   6   5   4   3

Cover images © jippu2498/123RF.

This book is available at quantity discounts for bulk purchases.
For information, please call 1-800-289-0963.

Contents

Acknowledgments

I would like to thank my wife Lourdes and my son Christian for always lending support. And thanks to Grace Freedson as always. No Grace, no gigs. Caffeine and my MP3 playlists get a nod, too.

Top 10 Tips That Will Keep You in the Money

1. Never stop trying to get better at investing. Never stop learning about how markets work. Take courses. Read books. Ask questions. And don't be afraid to admit that you've made a mistake. Mistakes, which can cost you some money, are the things that teach us how to become better investors.

2. Set realistic goals. If you have $1,000 to get started, then don't expect to quit your job one month into your investment life.

3. Be specific, detailed, and disciplined about what you will set aside for investment, how often you will invest it, and how you will monitor your success.

4. Be a penny pincher. Before you think of investing, make sure you have enough money set aside to get started and never stop adding to your account.

5. Be patient and picky. If an investment does not meet your strict criteria, skip it. You may miss a great opportunity but you'll be able to sleep at night.

6. Stay plugged in. Never skip a day when you don't know the big picture in your investments. If you own stocks or stock mutual funds, you should, at the very least, know how the stock market closed every day.

7. Never assume anything. Always figure it out for yourself. Don't be intimidated by data or talking heads on TV, radio, and the Internet. If you don't get or believe what they're saying, go research it. Figure it out for yourself.

8. Never follow hot tips. A hot tip is usually old news or insider trading. Either way you lose.

9. Get a daily routine. Once you find something that works, stick with it. Read the same paper. Go to the same websites. Drink the same drink. At the same time, be true to yourself; if something is not working, it's time to change it.

10. If you don't enjoy investing, maybe you should consider an investment advisor.

Introduction

EVERY DECADE OR SO, the economic cycle turns and the prevalent trend shifts the other way. In the 1990s, recession gave way to the Internet boom, which eventually came crashing down. The twenty-first century was all about real estate and housing, until that market fizzled and burned. Every boom and bust creates a new set of challenges and opportunities, especially for those who understand the dynamics of markets and how to navigate them.

Yet, many people don't realize that knowledge, preparation, patience, and realistic expectations are the key to being a successful investor. If you throw in a dash of good humor and add the fact that you are young, the odds of maximizing your potential for building wealth are on your side. You can invest in stocks, bonds, and real estate. And you can, if you know what to look for and how to plan accordingly, both profit on the way up, and protect your gains while minimizing losses when the trend eventually turns.

Change is inevitable. Markets will rise and fall. The political landscape will change, often very dramatically in moderate periods of time. And life will go along with the change. Yet, if you observe, learn, plan, adjust, and make sound decisions, you will likely be much better off with your investments than if you just try to fly by the seat of your pants or simply hope for the best. Too many times people will make hasty decisions about investments based on tips, whims, or impulse.

If the market is rising, everyone is happy. When markets fall, the average person just tends to hope that things will get better. If things don't, people abandon investing altogether. Don't get discouraged. The fact is that you can manage your losses. You can make money if the markets fall. And you can, with a certain degree of accuracy, predict and prepare for significant changes of direction in the market.

This book is about getting organized, how to gather information, and how to participate, based on your risk profile, in the stock, bond, and real estate markets. It's about having a long-term plan, but also how to adjust your plan. It's about getting to know your own willingness to take risk and how to manage your risk. And it's all about choosing investment classes, such as stocks, bonds, real estate, and mutual funds, and how to put them together in an asset allocation mix that makes sense for you. It's also about how to save for your retirement and your child's education. More importantly, it's designed and written with one single goal: to guide you to build your wealth without guesswork and anguish.

In the end, time is on your side. If you start investing in your 20s and 30s, you will have ample opportunities to build the kind of financial future that you are looking for. Get started. Time's a wasting.

CHAPTER 1

Are You Ready to Become an Investor?

If current socioeconomic trends continue, people of all ages will need to contribute more of their own money toward their retirement. If that process seems daunting, consider the fact that the longer you put off getting started investing, the harder it may be to build enough of a nest egg to make life easier in the future. So in order to be ready, it's important to understand the big picture. Investing is the long-term process by which you build wealth, and has two basic components—saving and compounding. Saving is the act of putting money away for the purpose of investing. Compounding is what money does for you by earning interest, and by the price appreciation of your investments, or both. Together these two processes grow your money. Once you understand these concepts, you are ready to get started.

Can You Afford to Invest?

You have to start somewhere. At the early stages of the investing process important questions should be raised. Simply stated: Investing without money is like quenching thirst without water. Start by asking the question of whether you can "afford" to invest. By doing that you've made some progress, as other important questions will follow.

How Will You Finance Your Investing?

The money you use for investing can come from anywhere—a savings account, an inheritance, or even a lottery win. For most people, investment money is money earned from a job or profession. If you've got some money already put aside, you're ahead of the game. The more you have, the better your starting point. The least desirable money source to start an investing plan is to get a loan, as that would start your investment plan at a deficit.

ESSENTIAL

Build your savings first. Billionaires build their fortunes by owning and managing their businesses. The stock market is a place where they preserve the purchasing power of their fortunes. For example, Warren Buffett, through his company Berkshire Hathaway, owns businesses such as Geico and General Reinsurance Corporation. He uses the profits from his businesses to buy stock in other companies like Coca-Cola. That way he diversifies his holdings, but also earns dividends and price appreciation from the stock market.

A simple way to figure out if you can afford to invest is to count how much money you have left at the end of the month after all your bills are paid. If it's $100, that's as good a place to start as any, and that is money that will be put to good use by saving it in a bank account or a money market mutual fund. A money market mutual fund is a special type of mutual fund that invests in short-term interest paying bonds (maturity of less than 90 days) such as U.S. government treasury bills or what is known as commercial paper (similar short-term bonds issued by corporations). Think of a money market mutual fund as a holding tank for your money while you decide what to do with it. If it's less than $100, it means that you need to work a little harder at controlling your expenses.

Still, $50 is better than nothing. It makes good sense to have at least $1,000 saved before you make a move such as buying shares in a mutual fund that invests in stocks or bonds, which is a good entry-level place for investors. If it was easy to save $100 the first month, get greedy and go for $200 next month, so you can grow your nest egg more quickly.

If you don't have extra money at the end of the month, there is no point in trying to invest yet. In that case, your first step should be to trim your expenses. If you're trying to make money without some kind of backing, you're asking for trouble. So, don't put your rent or food money into a mutual fund; you may find yourself without a place to live or going hungry.

ALERT

Pay off as much debt as possible before you start investing. Debt is a drag on your ability to save. Think of debt as a big sack of potatoes that you carry on your back everywhere you go. By paying debt you are taking that big weight off of your financial shoulders. Being lighter makes you move faster.

Details Are Important

Successful investors are very specific about what they are going to do and how they are going to do it. For example, plan what you will set aside for investment, how often you will invest it, and how you will monitor your progress. As time passes and your investments grow, make changes if needed. Consider revisiting your goals and your expectations. A reliable plan in the early stages of investing is to set aside at least $100 per month until you get to $1,000. While you are saving money to invest, you should also be researching different mutual fund companies to find out which one makes more sense to you. Some of the more popular and reliable mutual fund companies are Fidelity Investments (*www.fidelity.com*), The Vanguard Group (*https://investor.vanguard.com/home*), and T. Rowe Price (*www.troweprice.com*).

The major reasons most small investors fail is that they don't have a lot of cash and that they risk too much too soon. That means that they don't have enough money around to get them through tough times. That is also the most common reason people give up on investing. Markets go up and markets go down. So in order to stay in the game, set aside as much as you can before you try to put it to work and then keep adding as much as you can as often as possible. That's how you will make the most out of compounding.

Know Your Risk Profile

Knowing how much you are willing to risk in investments is a tricky business, as it depends on both your personality and your ability to be objective based on your circumstances. If you are willing to jump out of an airplane without a parachute, you might like to trade options and futures without doing your research or doing some paper trading without risking real money. That's crazy. But by the same token, people who don't like to leave their house if there are clouds in the sky don't make good investors either.

Still, it makes sense to know what your tendencies are. Once you know, you can explore the different kinds of investments and methods that may make sense for you. Regardless of your risk profile, as an investor there is no substitute for planning, study, risk understanding, and patience.

What's the best way to figure out your risk profile? Ask yourself these three questions:

- How much can I afford to lose?
- How much do I need to reach my goals?
- How do I react to losing?

If you only have a few hundred dollars to your name, and you need them to get by, you should avoid high-risk investments and concentrate on saving money that you will invest in the future. If your goal is to have a million dollars by the time you retire and you are only twenty-three years old, time is on your side. In this case, everything depends on how much money you can save over time and how well that money can be invested in order to maximize the savings and compounding dynamics. If you get sick to your stomach and pull your hair out when your favorite football team loses a game, lower-risk investments may be the way to go for you, especially when markets become volatile in response to an international event that is well beyond your control.

ESSENTIAL

If you are uncomfortable with an investment, consider taking other steps to remove your uncertainty. You may want to research the investment further before making a decision on whether to own it. You may want to invest in another investment class altogether or choose another vendor. If stocks are not for you, consider real estate, bonds, or even something like investing in a franchise and building a business. There are many different asset classes and investment opportunities, each one with its own set of risks and potential rewards. Finally, if you own something and it's not going well, it may be best to get out of the position. A good rule to follow is that if you don't understand it, you shouldn't invest in it.

Setting Realistic Goals and Timetables

Your timetable starts when you decide to start investing. Your first step is to decide when you will open your account and how much you will put in it. If you have money set aside, you're ahead of the game. If you have less than $1,000, it makes sense to put that money in the bank or in a money market mutual fund and continue adding to the account until you have enough to start investing. Avoid putting that money in a CD (certificate of deposit) or another type of account that won't allow you to add to it or that will limit how often you can put money in or take it out.

Put It in Writing

Wishing for something won't help you get it, but writing your goals on paper, reading them frequently, and reviewing and refining them will get you places. The more specific you are, the better off you'll be. Note the goal, the time frame to reach the goal, the amount of money you'll need, how much you have now, and what you are willing to do to get to your goals.

If your long-term goal is to retire early, write down the age of retirement, where you'd like to live, and how much money you think you'll need. Write it in such detail that you can see yourself doing it. "I want to retire when I'm fifty. I want to move to Cape Cod and live in a house by the shore with a great view of the sea. I plan to do a little consulting work on the side and run along the beach with my dog every day." Experience this fully every time you look at your sheet of paper or your smartphone. If you have shorter-term goals, like owning a home or visiting a specific foreign country, include those as well and divide your savings and investing capital between them.

Break the process down into stages. Set monthly, quarterly, and yearly goals. Be specific. Write down exactly how much you'll put into your IRA or 401(k) every month. Decide how much you'll pay in debt every month and to whom and how much money you will dedicate to each area. This process will require a great deal of time and planning, and it's likely to require adjustments along the way.

Review and Refine Your Plan

From time to time, see how much progress you're making. Do this on a monthly, quarterly, and yearly basis. Is your spouse or significant other participating in the plan? Does he understand the goals? If it's not going the way you planned, take a step back and review the situation. Give yourself credit for what you've accomplished and review where things didn't go as you planned. If your goals change, it's not a setback, just a reboot. Go through the same process of planning for your next goal.

Talking things over with friends or relatives may also be helpful. If what you're doing isn't working, it may be time to get a second opinion. Successful people are usually willing to lend a helping hand to those in need. By raising the issue with someone who's been there, you may discover that your problem isn't as big as you think. The answer may be something as simple as getting a recommendation for a good advisor who is willing to be your consultant or the name of a good investment club.

Find some good online resources for retirement planning and personal finance, like MarketWatch.com's personal finance and retirement sections (*www.marketwatch.com/personal-finance?link=MW_Nav_PF* and *www.marketwatch.com/retirement?link=MW_Nav_Retirement)*. The personal finance section offers great ideas for budgeting, saving money on credit cards, how to get bargain trips, and great general tips on how to save money. The retirement section is terrific for getting organized and staying updated on changes in mutual funds, IRA rules, and what to do with your 401(k) plan. The key is to continue to plan and save no matter what.

How Much Will You Need to Get Started?

Theoretically, you can start with a nickel. But in the real world, the more you have when you start investing, the better off you'll be. What's even more important is how much you'll need to save and invest over time. A rule of thumb used by some mutual fund companies is that you should save eight times your annual ending salary, the money that you have after taxes and expenses, in order to retire. It's not likely that a young person can do that right away, so it can be done in a stepwise fashion.

ALERT

Searching through the free content on a mutual fund or bank website can give you a fair amount of useful information. Just beware of the fact that their goal is to get you to invest your money with them. Make sure that you use the information that is sensible without necessarily buying into a sales pitch.

For example, if you start at age twenty-five and you save one time your ending salary by the time you're thirty-five, the next goal should be to save three times your ending salary by the time you're forty-five, five times by the time you're fifty-five, and so on. Remember, this is just a formula. Life isn't always this neat, but you do have a benchmark. You can modify this formula by starting to save earlier or retiring late. You can also try to put more money away every chance you get. If you have a 401(k) plan as your main retirement source, max that out and start a separate IRA to add more money to your retirement.

Always Think Liquid

You've got some savings; you've got a plan; and you're looking for ways to get things moving. One of the most useful things to do when investing is to consider the flexibility or liquidity of any investing vehicle. Liquidity is the ease of moving the money around. And it comes in handy if something changes, such as a sudden short-term price drop in the stock market that gives you an opportunity to buy shares at lower prices. Let's say that you get a side job that pays quickly or you get a bonus or a raise at work. Suddenly you have extra money. That extra money could take you to your $1,000 initial investment target, letting you start your investing plan sooner than you might have intended. If your savings is locked up in a CD that won't let you move the money around for six months or a year, you'll be stuck and will have to wait until the CD matures before you can get started on your longer-term investment plan.

Bank Accounts Versus Money Market Mutual Funds

Bank accounts and money market mutual funds are the most liquid savings and investing vehicles. And although they are similar, they are not the same. You set up a bank account with a bank and you open the money market mutual fund with a brokerage or mutual fund company. Savings accounts pay interest rates. Checking accounts sometimes pay interest. Money market mutual funds pay interest rates and have check writing privileges, but they often require as much as $1,000 minimum balance, and some may limit the number of checks that you can write from the account. Therefore, a good rule is to have a bank account for savings and paying bills and a money market mutual fund as the central holding area for investment capital.

FACT

The big mutual fund companies, including Fidelity, Vanguard, and T. Rowe Price, all have money market mutual funds. Get the information online or by calling their toll-free phone number. Review the prospectus. Compare several money market funds and fund companies before making a final decision. Your bank may offer a money market mutual fund. Unfortunately, many banks will have higher fees and more hidden fees with worse investment returns than the mutual fund companies. Consider this if your bank starts pitching its investments to you.

Open a money market mutual fund account as your initial investment decision. This account will serve as your central investment account. From there you can switch money to mutual funds, stocks, and other investments with a phone call or a click of your mouse.

Next, you'll decide how much money you'll set aside for investing and how often you will add to your investments. A good method is to add at least a certain amount every month. If your goal is $100 every month, but you only have $50 this month, add the $50. Try to add $150 next month. Just keep adding to your account.

ALERT

> Separate your savings from your investments. Once you have enough money to invest, split your funds between a bank savings account and a mutual fund/brokerage money market account. You need to have some money in the bank for emergencies so that you don't have to tap your investment account unless it is absolutely necessary.

Give yourself a checkup every three months. If you're not where you thought you should be, ask yourself why and do your best to make it right. You can adjust your timetable to conform to your circumstances. If you lose your job, that will make things difficult. But if you get a promotion and a raise, give your investment account a raise, too, and modify your addition schedule.

When you reach a milestone, as in when you get to your first $10,000, see what you can do to get to $20,000 faster than you got to $10,000. Do it again when you get to $30,000. Always give yourself room for error, but always make changes looking to make your returns better. Investing is a fluid process. And those who keep up with what they are doing in a systematic fashion do better.

Know Before You Invest

Once you've opened your investment account, keep that money in the money market mutual fund as long as it takes for you to decide what to do with it. A money market account does not fluctuate in price. Although you are buying shares, each share is worth $1. That won't change unless very difficult financial circumstances develop. It's only happened once in the history of investing, during the 2008 financial crisis.

ALERT

The Federal Deposit Insurance Corporation (FDIC) does not insure money market mutual fund accounts. Money in these accounts is "at risk" of loss. The odds of losing money in a money market account are almost zero, though.

Once you've done some research, it may make sense for you to invest in a well-managed mutual fund that invests in stocks, bonds, or both (a balanced approach). If you know someone who had good results with a particular mutual fund, research it for yourself. Here's where talking to your mom, your dad, or an uncle or friend of the family with some money may come in handy.

ESSENTIAL

Build investment capital by putting money in your money market fund before you put it to work. By delaying transferring money directly into a stock or bond fund you are providing a cushion against potential losses and building up your cash reserves. This money may come in handy in the future, especially if the markets fall, giving you an opportunity to buy shares in your stock or bond fund at a cheaper price. You may be able to set up your money fund to automatically transfer money from your bank account. Bottom line: If you put $500 into your money market every month, only invest a portion that you are comfortable with, such as $250, in your stock or balanced mutual fund.

Don't bank on their advice too much, though. Get the prospectus and see for yourself. Explore how well the fund has done over time, and how well it's done recently. Start following its price on a weekly or daily basis for a few weeks. Always compare your funds, or your stocks, to the appropriate benchmark and to the general market. When you read a mutual fund prospectus it will always tell you which major stock index it is trying to emulate or beat. Most diversified growth or growth and income mutual funds will use the Standard & Poor's 500 (S&P 500) Index as a benchmark.

Once you get better at investing and start to invest in individual stocks, it's a similar dynamic to investing in a mutual fund, with a bit more detail. With a mutual fund you're investing in a management style, expertise, and investment strategy. With a company you're investing in the potential for profits. Yet, it's not that different. Get as much information as possible on the company. Ask people about their experience with the stock. Research the company and its products. Know its fiscal strategies, its management style, and review its future plans. For example: If you go to a coffee shop on a regular basis, it's always crowded, and it's part of a major chain like Starbucks, research the company. See how it's doing. And consider investing in it.

ESSENTIAL

When investing in individual stocks it's good to "kick the tires" before you buy. That means going to the supermarket and seeing if anyone is buying products made by that company or seeing how many cars are parked in the parking lot of a certain company that gets a lot of press in financial circles. Use this as the starting point for your research; then follow it by reviewing earnings and research reports, asking questions, and getting a long-term view of the company from a stock chart. You can find excellent stock charts on the web at *www.stockcharts.com*.

The Basics of Market Analysis

Individual investors have a responsibility to their future and their families. Investing is not a game. It's a serious activity that should be taken up only by those who wish to take it seriously, almost as a second occupation.

The Global Dynamic

There is now only one economy: the global economy. Commerce between companies, individuals, and countries is now synchronized.

Electronic payments and the instantaneous flow of information through cell phones and the Internet make for very fast responses to news and money.

Within the global economy, there are four basic investment markets: stocks, bonds, commodities, and real estate. Each individual market responds to variables in its own country's economy, as well as to various external influences, such as changes in interest rates or in major economic regions around the world such as the United States, China, or Europe.

It's also not uncommon to see U.S. stocks react to important economic data from China or Germany, such as changes in Gross Domestic Product or other key economic variables. This is because U.S. companies sell products all over the world, and economic growth or contraction in the other economies of the world can affect the future profits of U.S. companies.

Central Banks and Markets

Central banks are government banks that function to monitor and respond to the economies of their country by raising or lowering interest rates. In general, weakening economies lead central banks to lower interest rates. Economies that show so much strength that inflation is starting to rise lead to higher interest rates.

The most powerful influence on global financial markets is the direction of interest rates. The U.S. Federal Reserve is considered the world's most influential central bank. The bond market moves in response to the actions of the Federal Reserve and other central banks, and the other markets eventually follow.

As a general rule, lower interest rates are good for stocks and bonds, because stock and bond prices tend to rise in response to lower interest rates. Commodities, such as gold, oil, wheat, corn, and coffee, and gasoline prices respond less to interest rates and are more influenced by supply and demand as well as the general state of the world's political climate. Real estate responds to both interest rates and supply and demand for land and housing.

Each one of these markets has its own set of dynamics and should be known and understood both as an individual place to invest as well as how it's behaving in response to the others, to interest rates, to inflation, and to the global political situation at any time.

Political Influences

Politics often lead to market volatility. Wars, disputes, and agreements between nations can affect all markets because all markets are now interconnected around the world. It is possible for any investor to invest in just about anything, anywhere, at any time, through direct investments, such as stocks and bonds, or through mutual funds.

Keep in mind, though, that events in Ukraine, Indonesia, Baghdad, or Beijing can and will affect your personal investments. The world of the twenty-first century is connected. News travels fast. Money moves at the touch of a button. All markets are interconnected. And risk can go from a very low level to a place of extreme danger in a few minutes. All investors should become "experts" in their chosen investment fields to the extent that they can be aware of the risk of losses.

Evaluate and Adjust Your Approach

Take a step back and consider your options. This chapter is about making decisions, getting basic information, and taking the basic steps to start investing. You should have the tools now to know if you're ready to become an investor and how to get started.

There is an orderly method for getting started with investing, with a beginning, middle, and endpoint. The three basic steps are asking questions, letting the answers lead to the next step, and getting used to the notion that frequent evaluation is the way to keep things going in the right direction.

Writing your plan down, keeping it handy, and reading it on a regular basis reinforces your goals, letting your subconscious mind do its job, which is to process information and eventually help you to make better decisions. By paying attention to the markets on a regular basis you will improve your understanding of how they work, and by checking how your investments respond to the action in the markets you will get a good feel as to what works and what doesn't.

The "Ready to Invest" Test

Before investing, make sure you've got these areas covered:

1. Have steady income
2. Have money left over after meeting your obligations
3. Consider the effect of upcoming personal changes such as marriage, children, or divorce before investing
4. Build savings before establishing an investment capital fund
5. Use a money market mutual fund as your platform for investing
6. Know your risk profile
7. Do your homework before investing in anything
8. Invest in mutual funds before investing in stocks

CHAPTER 2

Steps to Grow Your Nest Egg

Every investor needs a source of investment capital. This is often called the nest egg, and it is central to your investment plan. This chapter is about starting, growing, and using your nest egg for investing. More than a holding tank, the nest egg is both a launching and a landing pad. Money will come into it, earn interest, and be deployed based on the overall plan.

Give Your Finances a Physical

Optimize your nest egg by first taking an honest inventory of your finances. Make two lists: "Sources of Income" and "Expenses." Be as specific as possible in both of them. First, make a list of your sources of income:

- Wages from your job(s)
- Bonuses
- Child support or alimony
- Rental income
- Interest income
- Dividend income
- Capital gains income
- Other income

Next, list your expenses. This list may be larger than the income list. Include every possible expense that you can think of in your initial expenses list. You can always pare it down later. Here are some sample expense categories:

- Savings
- Mortgage or rent
- Utilities
- Car payment
- Other
- Public transportation
- Credit card payments
- Student loans
- Any other loan payments
- Home maintenance
- Child care
- Child support or alimony
- Insurance: car, health, home, other(s)
- Out-of-pocket medical expenses
- Health insurance if self-employed
- Computer expenses
- Cell phone

- Entertainment/recreation
- Food: dining out/groceries
- Clothing and shoes
- Gifts and donations
- Hobbies
- Interest expense
- Household/personal care products
- Federal, state, and local income tax
- Social security tax
- Property tax
- Retirement contributions
- Investments
- Pet expenses

This is a great exercise as you'll be surprised at what you spend and where you spend it. The purpose of this checkup is to help you find places where you can make good decisions, create a good budget, and free up money for investments. Consider what you spend on subscriptions (online and off), and holiday, birthday, and anniversary gifts. Given the amount of free information on the Internet, you may not need some of those magazine subscriptions. Maybe you need to cut back on how much you spend on gifts for others as well.

ESSENTIAL

Use as many sources of data as possible to do your financial physical exam. Include credit card statements, loan statements, receipts, and your checkbook. By including as many expenses as possible, you will get the most complete picture and you'll give yourself the best chance of success when you start preparing your budget.

Savings and investments are included as expenses. These are good things to include, as you will get an idea as to the percentage of your money that is already allocated to this area of your finances. Pay close attention to how much you are already putting into savings, your 401(k) plan, or an IRA. If you have zeros or minimal amounts next to these bullets, then you have your work cut out for you. But don't be discouraged. Every negative situation can be put to good use as an opportunity for improvement. Consider making a reduction in one of your "luxury" areas and taking that money and putting it in your 401(k) or IRA. You don't have to torture yourself, but maybe doing something like this every other month or once a quarter will work for you.

The Great Analysis

After you make your list, the next step is to evaluate its strengths and weaknesses. It's important to see where you're putting your money and consider the best use for it. Keep what makes sense and dump what doesn't work. If you're spending a lot of money on tennis lessons, but you're not getting to the pro tour, that's a sign that your tennis lesson money might be better spent on paying off some credit card debt, saving for retirement, or both. You may not be able to do the paying off or the saving as quickly as you like, but the mere fact that you've spotted it is huge because at the very least you've identified an opportunity for improvement.

It's a good idea to update the list you've made on a monthly basis and to see where there is progress and what needs work. Other areas that can easily be trimmed include entertainment expenses, such as movies. Matinees are cheaper than paying full price. You don't need to see every movie at the IMAX. And small popcorns and small drinks are likely better for your health than the often more expensive large ones. You don't have to go to the movies every week. In fact, sometimes Netflix may be cheaper. And books tend to be cheaper and are often more fun than movies. Be creative, and be true to yourself and your plan. Once you've analyzed your income and expenses, you can start to make a budget.

Artful Budgeting

It has been said that medicine is part art and part science. In many ways so is budgeting. There is no absolute way to budget, as much depends on the factors that affect each individual's life, income, spending habits, and overall circumstances. The one constant in budgeting is the goal: to trim expenses as much as possible in order to pay off debt and leave money for saving, investing, or other financial objectives, such as taking vacations, sending the kids to a special camp in the summer, or upgrading a home.

How Much Money Do You Have?

A good budget starts with knowing how much money you have available each month. That figure is the result of the physical exam you gave your finances, after subtracting expenses from income. It's a good idea to do this calculation based on figures for three months as you can start seeing some trends. What should emerge is a pretty good picture of where your money is going and how you can redirect it to better use.

Where Is Your Money Going?

You may discover that your finances are dying a slow death of losses via small expenses such as grocery shopping, cups of coffee, cigarettes, beer, wine, and going out to lunch and dinner with friends, add up and make the pain of the big expenses, like rent or mortgage, car payments, and loans, much worse.

Two packs of cigarettes per week cost somewhere around $40–$80 per month depending on where you live and what brand you smoke. That's $480–$1,000 per year. A daily $2 latte is $14 per week, $56 per month, and $672 per year. Tennis lessons can run $70–$100 per hour or more per week. That's $3,640 to $5,200 per year. That's somewhere between $5,000–$7,000 per year on stuff that you can reduce or cut out. You get the picture. The "little" things can add up in a hurry. By finding these small cuts, you can start to plan how to stop unnecessary spending.

Realistic Targeting of Expenses

Once you have a good idea where you are spending your money, you can start making some decisions about where to make adjustments. Divide your expenses into sections. Look at the big expenses first, then look at the medium expenses, and finally look at the smaller costs. The numbers will be different for everyone. The "bigs" may be those expenses that total above $300 per month and are likely to include rent or mortgage costs, car payments, and maybe some credit cards. The "mediums" may contain insurances and student loans—these would be the $50–$200 group—while the "smalls" should be those expenses below $50. The "smalls" will likely be the largest section and will include your cleaners bill, babysitters, groceries, movies, and other things that we often spend money on just because they happen to be convenient, or on impulse.

Separate the three groups of expenses and add them up as individual categories. By putting numbers together with expenses, and then grouping them, you will get a better idea as to the effect each group is having on your finances and how to attack them. Mortgages, student loans, and car payments are likely to remain fixed costs. But there are plenty of other expenses that have the potential to be adjusted. That means that your biggest chances for spending cuts are likely to come from the "smalls." But that doesn't mean that you shouldn't spend time exploring the "bigs" and the "mediums." Here are two examples of how to look at your groups, ranging from big to small:

In the "big" column, a $2,000 credit card balance at 13% interest per year, on which you're only making minimum payments every month, while you continue to charge, could turn into a $3,500 balance in five years, assuming that the interest rate stayed the same. If interest rates rise, you would pay more. Consider targeting the credit card debt as your first success in order to free up money for saving and investing. If you pay that credit card off and instead save $3,500, it could grow to nearly $4,500 in five years at 5% compounded interest.

FACT

Consider switching to a zero interest rate credit card. You will pay a "fee" up front, but you will usually have a year to pay off the card balance at a lower interest rate. This will free up money that can be used to pay other expenses, to put toward savings and investment, or both.

In the "small" column is grocery shopping. A larger than expected "surprise" here may be from buying prepared foods, which cost more. Start buying fresh food and cook it yourself more often. Snacks are also expensive and can be cut back. Sodas, flavored water, and "coffee" drinks add up, too. Consider going to the grocery store more often and buying only what you need each time, instead of making one big monthly trip where you might buy more than you really need of any one item. Set concrete spending targets on your choices, and pinpoint the things that won't hurt as much as others. If nightly dining out is standing out as a big expense, cut the five nights of dinner out per week to one or two and use the nights out as treats for making a good decision.

Intangible Benefits

Think outside the box as there may be more benefits besides freeing up some money when you make some spending cuts. In turn, those "extra" benefits may have a positive impact on your budget. By cooking your own food you are more likely to be eating fresh, less processed food. There are clear health benefits to be gained from this, which may translate into lower medical expenses.

If you spend $30 per month on public transportation, it may make sense to walk more. Do you really need to hail that cab? If you take the subway, consider walking one stop farther before taking the train. Walking is good exercise, and the token may cost less if you buy it three blocks farther along. If you can walk to work, it may be worth it to take that thirty-minute walk and the thirty-minute walk home every day.

Look for free stuff when you treat yourself. If you buy Starbucks coffee by the bag at the grocery store, there is a coupon for a free cup of coffee at the bottom. That can add up to twenty or more free cups of coffee per year if you're a regular customer.

Shop for your cell phone plan. You may find significant savings as often as twice per year when the plans do updates or service upgrades. Sometimes they'll throw in a free phone. A $20 per month savings will bring you $240 per year.

FACT

It pays to shop and to read the label. A 31-ounce jar of store brand salted peanuts costs $5.99, while the 32-ounce jar of the popular brand costs $7.99. Two dollars is a lot of money to pay for an ounce of peanuts. If the store peanuts are just as good, or close to the national brand in flavor and consistency, this is an easy choice. It makes sense to compare similar products and to try different strategies.

See the Difference

The next step is to compare how much money you will spend after your analysis and your targeted cuts. Whatever is left is your net income, or what you will put in your bank account or your money market mutual fund in order to build your savings and investing capital fund. Track this figure over three months and see where things stand.

ALERT

You need a name for the money you will use to invest. Consider calling it your "investing capital fund." It's a good descriptive term, but it's also a sign that you are starting to get in the right mindset and you are becoming a more serious investor.

If you've made good decisions based on your financial checkup and your analysis of the data, and have begun to artfully budget, you should start seeing some of your debt shrink, and you should be noticing that what's left in your pocket has grown each month. Even if it's a small amount, such as $50, it's progress. As you pay more things off, like credit cards, if you control your expenses, and you adjust your objectives, your net income should start to grow along with your investing capital fund.

Personal Finance Software and Apps

You can spend money on software like Quicken, or you can use an Excel spreadsheet. If you're trying to save money, the spreadsheet may be the way to go. If you want to plan for the future, or centralize your finances, software often lets you do your budget, do your taxes online, as well as write checks and pay bills. You may want to do a spreadsheet at first and then move up to the software as you get better. The important thing is to get organized and to give yourself the ability to track your budget and to gauge your successes and failures so that you can make changes as needed.

Start with the simple entries and add details as you progress. Balancing your checkbook and paying bills is a good beginning. It will get you comfortable with the software and help you to develop a routine. The data you enter into the software will also become the basis for your budgeting.

ALERT

Your bank or investment firm may have free financial and budgeting software available on its website. This may be all you need to get started before you spend money on other software or apps.

Personal finance software helps you get organized, as it has built-in templates that can save you time and effort as you plug in data. It also has graphing and trending functions, which lets you see your progress over time.

You can buy Quicken at *www.intuit.com*. Another popular software for budgeting is Mint, found at *www.mint.com*; for Moneydance, hit *www.money dance.com*. All three software packages can be found at *www.amazon.com*. The basic version of each software package costs between $30 and $40 after rebates.

Get Some Apps

For smartphone and mobile fans there are plenty of apps. Mint has free apps that you can download to iPhones, iPads, Android phones, tablets, and even Windows-based mobile devices. Ireconcile, *www.imore.com*, costs $1.99 per month or $19.99 per year, has extensive reporting capacity, and offers online backup. There are others as well, such as MoneyBook, Toshl, and Expenditure, that are free or can be purchased from iTunes, *www .itunes.com*.

Some of the great features that these apps offer include real-time data capacity, the ability to roll over money that you have left in one month to your next month's budget, and cloud storage. Some even have currency conversion capacity and the ability to associate a photo or note with your financial entry.

Develop a Progress Checklist

Update your budget on a monthly basis, as early as possible after you have all the data. By starting early you have a chance to make adjustments that will show up sooner. Use all the information possible. Include data from your checkbook, bank and credit card statements, and receipts. Make the changes in your spreadsheet or your budgeting software and consider graphing it over time. A picture really is worth a thousand words.

Adjust the List as Needed

This is a fluid process. You may miss your targets in some areas and exceed them in others. If you miss the numbers altogether, don't be discouraged. That just means that you have to re-examine what you're doing and make more adjustments. You may have too much detail and may need to combine some categories or rethink your priorities. There is no absolute way to do this, especially if your circumstances change. Small changes can add up, so look for easy places where you can cut spending without causing yourself too much pain.

Any time there is a significant change in your life, it will affect your budget. Getting married, changing jobs, changes in salaries, having a child, having to take care of a loved one, and many other inevitable events can affect how you spend your money and will have to be adjusted.

Leaks and Consequences

When adjusting your list, spend some time looking for leaks. These are those little expenses that can add up without you noticing, but can cause a good deal of damage to your budget. Spending leaks come mostly from impulse buying of things that you didn't realize that you "needed." Much of the time this kind of buying is influenced by advertising and is best avoided as it can ruin your budget. If you fall prey to this kind of situation on a regular basis it will make reaching your goal more difficult.

The best way to plug the leaks is to only buy what you need. If you go grocery shopping, make your list beforehand and stick to it. If you buy things online, go to the item you need and don't fall for the "people who bought this also bought" ploy. If you're buying a book that costs $20 and there is an offer for buying a second book for $15, it's best to avoid it. Even though spending $35 for two books may sound good, in real terms, you spent $15 on impulse. That's $15 that could have gone elsewhere. If you fall for this kind of thing on a regular basis, it will add up. Be strong.

Don't Quit

Making a budget and sticking to it can be discouraging. It's natural, when your goal is to invest, to want to jump right to it. But the hard truth is that you need capital to save and invest, and the most likely source for it is your income and what you do with it.

That means that you need patience and motivation.

FACT

Single people can make budgeting and investment decisions faster. Those with families have to consider spouses and children. Consider their needs. Ask for their input. Sometimes it makes more sense to buy the store brand of an item than to cut it out completely. Just by making this change, the savings can be significant.

Try to make the budget as simple as possible. If you have a family, make it a team effort. Reward yourself for hitting a milestone, such as when you have your stated goal for investing at the end of the month or when you pay off a credit card. There is a good feeling when you've made progress, and success tends to bring more success.

Remember that your budget is a means to an end. It's a useful tool. Don't lose sight of the goal, which is to have enough money left over at the end of the month to start an investing plan.

CHAPTER 3

A Quick and Dirty Overview of the Economy and Investment Vehicles

The economy is a complicated structure with a nearly infinite number of moving parts, which is why most people prefer not to think about it. As an investor, though, you will have to have a fair knowledge of how this big global beast works. You don't need a PhD in Economics, and you don't need to develop your own models. But it's helpful to have a good grasp on the big picture of economic activity at any one point in time and how it will affect interest rates and the return on your money, whether it's invested in stocks, bonds, mutual funds, real estate, commodities, or a combination of asset classes.

How Economic Activity Affects Everything

Think of the economy as a money generating machine and its accompanying distribution system. Things are made, grown, harvested, distributed, and eventually bought and sold by someone at some point. The economy is essentially the sum of all of those activities and transactions, and how the money that comes from those activities is deployed.

This is the quick and dirty of it. A strong economy expands. It generates jobs. Jobs lead to paychecks. Paychecks lead to purchases. Purchases lead to business expansion, more jobs, more paychecks, and so on. A weak economy contracts, leading to job losses and, in general, the reverse of what you see during good times.

ESSENTIAL

Economies can react to internal or external events. In 2008, the Great Recession occurred, which happened as external and internal events converged. In the 1990s, Congress repealed the post Great Depression laws that prevented investment banks from gambling with client money. That made the 2008 crisis worse since it not only led to losses for the banks, but also for investors and depositors. When real people's money joins big bank money in going down the drain, things are usually worse than if it's just one of the two.

Economic activity can go too far in both directions with significant consequences. If an economy expands too rapidly, it usually leads to inflation. That's when there is too much money available and not enough goods for purchase. That leads to increased demand and higher prices. A recession is the name for a period during which the economy contracts. This tends to be a time when there is too much supply of goods. It is a period where money, at least money in circulation used to buy things, expand businesses, create jobs, and so on, is scarce. Prices for goods and services often drop, or remain fairly stable, during a recession. When a recession reaches very low levels and job losses mount, it's often called a depression. A depression is a grim period of history where there is a great deal of suffering. The hallmark of a depression is the inability of people to find work.

In the Great Depression there was widespread unemployment, with the peak unemployment rate reaching 25 percent in 1933. In comparison, during the Great Recession or between 2007–2009, the unemployment rate peaked at 10 percent in October 2009.

Economic Forecasting Is Inexact

Economic forecasting is very difficult, which is why economists are often referred to as "Dismal Scientists." This inexactness, or apparent unwillingness of the economy to follow the "rules" in a precise fashion, is easy to understand because at the very root of how economies function is human behavior. Human behavior is predictably unpredictable.

Generally, when people feel good about things they spend money. That drives economic activity. When things aren't going so well, they hold on to their money and economies tend to slow. The hard part is knowing when things go from good to bad and when things are back on the upswing. That's why it's best to keep any understanding of the economy in general terms and to understand that perfection in execution of investment strategy based on economic forecasting alone is nearly impossible.

What You Don't Know Could Hurt You

As an investor, it's good to know that the economy is hardest to gauge when its trends are changing. Markets can anticipate or respond to a change in the economy and will turn from one direction to another. A great bull market in stocks eventually rolls over and gives way to a bear market. At some point, there is economic correlation, meaning that a good or a bad stock market may come before or after it's apparent to economists and to the public that things have changed.

A bull market is when stock prices generally rise for extended periods of time, usually months to years. A bear market is the opposite. Generally, bull markets last longer than bear markets.

The key variable in knowing the fundamentals of the economy is that not all people will sense the same dynamic at the same time. Job losses, when economies soften, often start slowly and may remain undetected for some time. Meanwhile, investment trends, such as rising stock prices, may continue up to a point when job losses become more obvious or lead to a sudden decline in earnings for a key company. At that point, the stock market may take notice. The point is that it might take several months before a key change in the economy is noticeable, thus the reaction in stock prices may be sudden as the unknown becomes apparent. The same applies to every market.

Interest Rates Should Interest You

Interest rates are set by the Federal Reserve Bank in the United States, also known as the "Fed," and by other individual central banks around the world. Each central bank sets the rates for its own particular country or region. Central banks are government banks whose function is to monitor the economy and respond to changes in activity by raising or lowering interest rates. Congress mandates the U.S. Federal Reserve to "fight inflation" and to "maintain full employment." The Fed has a staff of economists, mathematicians, and professionals who spend all their time studying the economy and creating reports that provide the decision makers at the central bank with the data that leads them to make decisions about where to move interest rates.

Although there is no set formula for when the Federal Reserve makes a decision to raise or lower interest rates, the central bank generally changes interest rates when the rate setting committee agrees that the economy has slowed to the point where lower rates are needed, and when there is a danger of inflation and it needs to raise rates. The Federal Open Market Committee (FOMC) usually meets six to eight times per year to review data and make interest rate decisions.

Interest Rates Make the World Go Round

Interest rates, set by the Federal Reserve and other central banks, have a ripple effect through the economy, the markets, and your daily life. When the Fed changes any of its key interest rates, markets respond by adjusting prices. The ripple effects are changes in car loans, student loans, credit card interest rates, and mortgages. Anything that you buy on credit depends on the decisions made by the Federal Reserve.

ESSENTIAL

The Federal Reserve's decision-making body, the Federal Open Market Committee (FOMC), meets eight times per year, roughly every six weeks. The FOMC reports its decision on interest rates after every meeting, and the chairman holds a press conference after the decision is released. This decision and the press conference receive heavy press coverage and usually influence stock and bond prices. Catch the action on CNBC (*www.cnbc.com*). For more information and details on the Fed, go to *www.federalreserve.gov*.

The Federal Reserve has two important rates that you may hear mentioned in the news. The Fed Funds rate tells banks what to charge one another for short-term loans. The Discount Rate is the rate that the Fed charges banks to borrow from the central bank. Changes in either or both of these rates usually lead to important moves in the stock and bond market, with ripple effects to the economy.

How Interest Rates Affect Stocks and Bonds

As a beginning investor, the most important thing to understand is that the Federal Reserve and the major central banks in China, Japan, and the European Union have the power, by making changes to interest rates, to affect the value of your investment portfolio.

Generally, but not always, stocks tend to do well when the economy is doing well. The reason is that stocks, generally, reflect the fundamental aspects of companies. When the economy is doing well, stocks usually follow along as investors buy in order to participate in the trend toward rising earnings and profits of companies.

Bonds tend to do well when the economy is not doing so well. That's because inflation reduces the net return on bonds. The interest earned by bonds remains fixed and fixed returns can't compete with rising inflation. If a bond pays an interest rate of 5% and inflation is running at 2%, the net interest rate is 3%. If a bond pays 3% and inflation is rising faster, say at 4%, the return has been reduced to 1%.

Savings Accounts Don't Mind Higher Interest Rates

Rising interest rates aren't necessarily a bad thing. If you have a fair amount of money in a savings account or a money market mutual fund, the interest you earn on those savings will be higher as rates increase. Generally, money market mutual funds and savings accounts are low-risk investments, and earning a higher return with lower risk is a positive. If you have $1,000 in a money market mutual fund that is earning 3% per year, your return would be $30 per year. At 6% it would be $60 per year.

Mixed Blessings in Real Estate

Real estate also responds to interest rates. Lower interest rates lead to lower mortgage rates, which usually attract buyers. Higher interest rates do the opposite. Supply and demand for homes, especially new homes, also respond to interest rates. Builders borrow money to finance their business. As a result, lower interest rates tend to spur home building while higher interest rates tend to do the opposite. If you are a rental property owner, higher interest rates may be a good thing, as fewer people tend to buy homes and may decide to rent.

FACT

The average investment portfolio has both stock and bond investments. The purpose of allocating the money to different asset classes is to protect the investor against changes in the economy. The goal is to have the stock part of the portfolio rise in value during a strong economy and for the bond portion of the portfolio to decrease any potential losses from the stock portfolio if the economy and the stock market turn lower.

Important Numbers and Reports to Watch

There are a large number of economic reports released on a daily basis. Taken as a whole, cities, counties, and states release reports on a regular basis. The stock, bond, and commodity markets usually focus on the national reports released by key agencies of the federal government. There are five essential reports that no investor should be without knowledge of.

The Employment Situation Report

This is the granddaddy of them all. Also known as the Jobs Report, this key set of data is released by the U.S. Government Bureau of Labor Statistics (*www.bls.gov*) the first Friday of every month and usually leads to some kind of significant move in both the stock and bond market. It is especially important near elections or during heated political periods as both Republicans and Democrats, in Congress and the White House, often make use of the data reported to further their political agendas.

ESSENTIAL

You can keep up with the schedule for report releases by logging on to the *Wall Street Journal*'s free calendar page (*http://online.wsj.com/mdc/public/page/2_3063-economicCalendar.html*).

The two big components are the number of new jobs created and the unemployment rate. The more new jobs that are created, the more likely the economy is expanding. The unemployment rate is a fuzzier number with some statistical nuances that tend to be negligible for most investors. Generally, a low unemployment rate is a positive.

Consumer Price Index (CPI)

This is a monthly report, which is released by the U.S. Government Bureau of Labor Statistics (*www.bls.gov*), that measures inflation at the consumer level, or what people pay when they buy things. It's used by the Federal Reserve as one of its data points for making changes in interest rates. The Fed has an inflation target. If the CPI number starts to move above where the Fed thinks it should, it is a signal that higher interest rates may be on their way. A lower than expected CPI may be a signal that the economy is slowing and that demand for goods and services is falling. A falling CPI may be a signal that the Federal Reserve will decide to lower interest rates. The stock and bond market pay very close attention to this number if it is above or below expectations.

Gross Domestic Product (GDP)

Gross Domestic Product is another monthly report released by the U.S. Department of Commerce Bureau of Economic Analysis (*www.bea.gov*). GDP is a big picture item that reports on the sum of all the goods and services produced in the United States. It's a snapshot of how much the economy grew on a quarterly and yearly basis. It's expressed as a percentage. A figure of 4% or above is considered healthy while 2% or below is seen as slowing. Two consecutive quarters or more of negative growth (below zero) is the definition of a recession.

GDP is not always as big a market mover as the Jobs Report, unless there is a surprise. For example, if the markets were expecting 3% growth, but the actual figure is 5.2% growth, that means that the economy is growing at a much faster rate than expected. Stocks, bonds, and maybe even the Federal Reserve would respond. What direction the response turns, up or down, would depend on where the market cycle is at the time. The response to a surprising report, GDP or otherwise, is an example of the inexact nature of economic forecasting and of the behavior of markets.

Institute for Supply Management Report (ISM)

The Institute for Supply Management's Report on Business Manufacturing Data (*www.ism.ws/ismreport/mfgrob.cfm*) is a private sector report that usually moves the market. The focus is on the Purchasing Managers Index (PMI). If this index is above fifty, the manufacturing economy is considered to be growing. A number below fifty is considered indicative of economic contraction. The PMI has eight components. Each of them is given a value. The eight numbers are then placed into the formula that gives the overall PMI number. Generally, a "good" number (above fifty, or if below fifty, one that is rising) is considered a positive.

The ISM was established in 1915 and its purpose is to provide information, education, and guidance to supply management professionals. PMI components are: new orders, production, employment, supplier deliveries, inventories, customers' inventories, prices, backlog of orders, exports, and imports.

FACT

The ISM also produces a nonmanufacturing report that focuses on the service economy. This report is not always as influential as the manufacturing data report but can be a market mover.

The Beige Book

This report is the product of all the information gathered by the Federal Reserve about the economy for the previous six weeks. It's based on interviews and research done by the Fed staff in each of the central bank's twelve district banks (*www.federalreserve.gov/otherfrb.htm*). The full text can be found at the Fed's website upon release. CNBC, Bloomberg, and Fox Business news all spend a good deal of time reporting on the information in each installment. The market usually responds, often significantly, based on the information. Each installment reports on economic activity in each of the districts in detail and often provides quotes and other important notes about the general and detailed economic activity, as well as future plans by businesses with regard to the economy.

Why the Rest of the World Matters

Globalization, or the near synchronization of the global economy, has had both positive and negative effects on investors. One good part of globilzation is the fact that companies can make money more easily throughout the world. In general, this has increased the potential to grow their earnings and to increase jobs. Most importantly, it has increased the potential for profit for investors. The downside is that the world can be a dangerous place. Anything can happen out there, from crazy weather to terrorist attacks to political upheaval, all of which affect the economy.

As the 2008 financial crisis proved, the near collapse of the banking system in the United States spread throughout the world. European, Chinese, Japanese, Russian, South American, and Middle Eastern banks and investors experienced large amounts of losses. The danger to the global financial system was the highest that it had been since the Great Depression in 1929.

The bottom line is that globalization has increased risk for all companies, whether they are based in the United States or elsewhere. Higher risk means that earnings can suffer and the volatility of a portfolio can increase as a result. Risk, unfortunately, can be managed but not avoided. And the understanding that it is a daily presence for any investor is paramount. What happens to your investments happens to you.

Stocks, Bonds, and Mutual Funds

Think of stocks, bonds, and mutual funds as three different ways to participate in the fortunes of a company, or in the case of a bond, in the fortunes of a company or a government or government entity. The difference between a bond and a stock is that bonds are IOUs while stocks are pieces of a company. A mutual fund is an investment company that invests in stocks, bonds, commodities, or a combination of several asset classes.

What Is a Stock?

Shares of stock are pieces of a company that give the holder the opportunity to participate in the fortunes of the enterprise, good or bad. These including price appreciation and dividends, as well as any potential losses that develop as a result of the decisions made by management, interest rates, or other external forces. Only the stock of public companies trades on exchanges or through some kind of over-the-counter arrangement as in the shares of penny stocks.

ALERT

A bad earnings report could ruin a small portfolio of stocks. If you own 300 shares of XYZ stock and it misses its earnings expectations, it could lose a large portion of its value in a hurry. If XYZ was 20% or more of your total portfolio, you could take a big haircut in a hurry.

Only investors with a good knowledge of the financial markets and a good-sized portfolio of at least $50,000–$100,000 minimum should consider investing in individual stocks. The reason for this is that individual stock prices tend to fluctuate more than mutual funds over time.

What Is a Bond?

Companies or governments sell bonds when they want to borrow money. Companies often borrow money through the bond markets in order to expand plants, develop new products, or to buy back bonds that pay higher interest rates and exchange them for bonds that pay lower interest rates. By selling bonds to investors, companies avoid or decrease upsetting their earnings streams, and are thus able to continue normal operations.

FACT

Bonds have two parts: the price and the yield. The price is what you would pay for the bond if you bought it. The yield is the interest rate that it pays. A bond quote involves both price and yield.

Governments sell bonds in order to pay off debt and to continue to fund their current and future obligations. The U.S. government finances its operations to a significant degree by selling U.S. Treasury Bonds, which are considered the highest-rated bonds in the world. Government agencies also sell bonds in order to keep enough capital around to keep making student loans without depending solely on taxpayers to foot the bill.

ESSENTIAL

News reports, especially regarding Treasury Bonds, focus on the yield or interest rate. When a news reporter says that bonds "are rallying," it means that interest rates are falling.

Why should anyone care about bond yields? Bond yields, especially the yield on the Ten-Year U.S. Treasury Note (TNX), are benchmarks for mortgages, car loans, home equity loans, and many other interest rates. It's good to know when bond yields fall, as it could be an opportunity to look into refinancing a mortgage or other loan.

What Is a Mutual Fund?

A mutual fund is an investment company that invests in assets on behalf of its clients. Investors buy shares in the mutual fund, not in individual assets or companies. Mutual funds have managers. Some mutual funds have a sole manager. Others are managed by committees of individuals and buy and sell assets based on the votes of the committee. Mutual fund managers are licensed by their states, and their actions are governed by the rules of the Securities and Exchange Commission. Fund managers are highly educated, often in finance as well as other fields of study. They have to pass rigorous examinations and are required, like all investment advisors, to attend continuing education classes and seminars. Companies that sell mutual fund shares to the public are highly regulated by the federal government.

ESSENTIAL

Consider buying your first mutual fund shares from a larger fund company that has been around for a long time. These companies tend to have better online and phone support and often sponsor seminars and classes for beginning investors.

Mutual funds offer a document called a prospectus, which lists the kinds of assets they invest in, the rules they follow, how they analyze the markets, their past performance, and most importantly, what they owned at the time the prospectus was filed.

Fundamental and Technical Market Analysis

There are two ways to analyze markets: technical and fundamental. The latter is the most common method, but not always the best, when used on its own. Fundamental analysis is all about facts and data. All earnings and economic reports, as well as news and events that affect prices, are considered fundamental analysis. A mutual fund prospectus, an opinion piece that you read on a financial website, and even going out and having a look around a retail store of a company that interests you, is considered fundamental analysis.

The advantage of this method is that you really get to know what you are investing in, which in the long haul is an excellent thing. The disadvantage is that company fundamentals don't always immediately correlate with the price of a stock or the direction of any market. And that's where technical analysis can help you make better decisions.

General Fundamentals of the Financial Markets

Fundamental data (the fundamentals) is the information that affects market behavior and direction: news items, economic releases, and events that happen on a regular basis. Each market—stocks, bonds, and commodities—has its own set of fundamentals. And while all markets have their own rhythm, because of globalization and the rapid spread of news via the Internet, all stocks, bonds, currencies, and commodity markets around the world are linked to one another. What happens in one market can, and often does, have repercussions in other markets.

If a positive U.S. Jobs Report leads to a rally in U.S. stocks, investors should expect similar moves in Asian and European markets on the next trading day. If you own a mutual fund that owns Japanese stocks, there is a good chance that it will have a good response.

What happens in stocks, bonds, and commodities can also affect the currency markets. At the same time, events that affect the U.S. dollar, the euro, and other world currencies can have positive or negative effects on stocks, bonds, and other financial markets.

QUESTION

Should beginning investors worry about the currency markets?
Beginning investors should be aware of the fact that currencies exist and that they may have an effect on their portfolios. Beginning investors should focus their energies on budgeting, paying off debt, and building an investment capital fund and deploying it.

Fundamentals of the Stock Market

The stock market is where stocks of companies trade. In the United States it is composed of three major indexes: The Dow Jones Industrial Average (INDU), the Standard & Poor's 500 (SPX), and the Nasdaq Composite Index (COMPQ). There are other well-known indexes, including the Dow Jones Transports Index (DJT) and the Dow Jones Utility Index (DJU). There are many more indexes as well. Most of them deal with individual sectors of the overall stock market, such as indexes that follow the prices in biotechnology and financial stocks.

An index is a group of stocks whose prices are worked through a formula to provide the value of the index at any one time. The Dow Jones Industrial Average has thirty stocks, and the price of the index at any time is what an investor would pay for one share of the index. So, if the Dow's most recent quote was 16,000, that's how much one share of the index would cost. The Standard & Poor's 500 (S&P 500) has five hundred stocks. The Nasdaq Composite houses over 4,000 stocks.

Company earnings, interest rates, and company mergers influence stock prices. External events, such as wars, changes in commodity prices, and trends in the bond market, also influence stock prices.

Fundamentals of the Bond Market

The bond market is much bigger than the stock market in terms of how much money exchanges hands there at any given time. It also has a much greater influence on the global economy than do stocks. While stocks often respond to economic trends, the bond market is often among the early influences on major economic trends. That's because bonds are all about interest rates, and credit depends on the general direction of interest rates. Generally speaking, rising interest rates slow economic growth while falling interest rates tend to stimulate growth.

ALERT

It is said that bond traders love bad news. Remember that bonds hate inflation. Inflation happens when economies grow too rapidly. A slowing economy is the best time to own bonds.

Technical Analysis

Technical analysis is a topic worthy of its own book. The bottom line is that it's based on reading and analyzing price charts. Beginning investors should know the basics. A picture, especially combined with good knowledge of the fundamentals, is really worth a thousand words. Here are the basic concepts that you can complement with an excellent tutorial that you can find at StockCharts.com (*http://stockcharts.com/school/doku.php?id=chart_school:chart_analysis*).

Price charts have three basic components: prices, moving averages, and other key points that let you get a good grip on whether this is a good time to enter or exit the market. To be sure, price charts can seem confusing at first glance. But by learning each individual section, anyone can know enough about them to get a good feel for whether the chart is flashing good or bad news, which is the most important aspect of technical analysis, to get a good feel for things and to compare the picture to the fundamentals.

If you're new to the study of price charts, this section gives you a tour of the essential information you'll need to glean useful information from them. Investors who focus solely or primarily on charts are known as chartists or technicians.

The First Look

The first look at a chart tells you a lot. Just by looking at the general direction, up or down, of prices, you get an idea as to what the action has been over any period of time you choose. Charts are divided into time periods. The most common periods cover the price action over one year with each period of the chart covering the price action for a day of trading.

Moving Averages

There are certain lines that traverse the page that are known as moving averages. Commonly used moving averages are the twenty-day, the fifty-day, and the 200-day moving average. Each moving average plots the average on prices for the number of days, ending on the last day plotted. Moving averages smooth out price action. A rising moving average is a positive factor for any financial instrument as it tells you that prices have trended higher for the past twenty, fifty, or 200 days.

Support and Resistance

Prices have important starting and stopping points. These are generally known as support and resistance. Support areas are where buyers tend to come in and buy. Resistance points are areas where sellers get the upper hand. Generally speaking, markets that find support are usually worth considering or buying into. Markets that find it difficult to move above resistance are usually worth avoiding or considering selling.

Volume

Charts also have vertical horizontal bars at the bottom. Volume counts the number of shares that rose and fell in the index on that day. Good charts have different colors for volume on up days and on down days. For example, prices on up days may be white while prices on down days may be red.

Generally high volume, up or down, especially over time, is a signal that the market is continuing to head in the direction of the volume. At some point volume reaches extreme levels, which can be a signal that the trend is about to reverse.

Investors that combine both fundamental and technical analysis have a more complete picture of where they are putting their money. Perhaps the best use of technical analysis is that it can be very helpful in choosing when to enter or exit any market. If you learn the few basic concepts of chart analysis, you will have a nice base to start from and will be able to make more informed decisions about your investments.

CHAPTER 4

A Close Look at Stocks

Stocks are a good place to start when you're a young investor because these are the investment vehicles that, over time, offer the most potential for portfolio growth. As with any other investment, individual stocks should be seen as part of a diversified portfolio, a part of their own market, as well as parts of a sector of industry. As you learn more, you should also consider what kind of a stock investor you may become: a shorter time frame–minded trader, a buy and hold investor, or somewhere in between.

The Exchanges

A stock exchange is a place where buyers and sellers meet to transfer shares to one another. The best-known stock exchanges are the New York Stock Exchange (the Big Board) and the Nasdaq. Generally, but not always, well-known nontechnology company shares tend to trade at the NYSE. More often than not, technology-related shares trade on the Nasdaq.

The NYSE still has floor brokers, known as specialists, who match orders from buyers and sellers. The Nasdaq is fully electronic, with market makers and their huge electronic platforms matching buyers and sellers. In reality, the NYSE is almost fully automated, but enough work is still done by people there.

There are other major stock exchanges around the world, such as the London Stock Exchange and the German Frankfurt Stock Exchange. Since the late twentieth century, many exchanges have either closed their doors or have merged into the larger exchanges. For example, the NYSE is actually part of a group called the NYSE Euronext.

Who Polices the Store?

The stock market, as do all large money enterprises, has the potential for fraud. The exchanges and industry associations such as the NASD (the National Association of Securities Dealers) do a fair amount of self-policing as do state-run securities boards. The big cop is the Securities and Exchange Commission (the SEC). The SEC has two main functions. First, its job is to enforce federal securities laws, investigate possible violations, and recommend solutions. Second, it must protect investors, especially small investors, from scams and from unscrupulous brokers.

On its website (*www.sec.gov*), the SEC provides free investment information, through its EDGAR (Electronic Data Gathering, Analysis, and Retrieval) database. You can find the latest public company reports, such as 10-Q and 10-K forms, that offer a look into the inside workings of companies. These forms often tell you about a company's upcoming plans, expectations, and more importantly, its concerns and potential difficulties.

QUESTION

Why do we need cops on Wall Street?
One of the most common crimes on Wall Street is insider trading. This is where someone who knows someone at a company gets information that is not available to the general public and uses it to buy or sell stock before the news breaks. The SEC investigates insider trading and other alleged illegal activities, such as high frequency trading (HFT) where traders who pay stock exchanges special fees get preferred data feeds and can make very fast trades using computers before the general public. HFT is not illegal, but its existence has become very controversial and is being heavily scrutinized.

What Stocks Really Are

Stocks are pieces of companies. When a company "goes public," the owners transfer pieces of the company in the form of shares to the public in what is known as an initial public offering (IPO). After the IPO, stocks trade on exchanges. By owning stock, an investor shares in the fortunes of the company, good or bad. These shares are known as common stock and give the shareholders rights, including the right to influence company policy and direction through votes at the annual shareholder meetings.

For example, in 2014 Google split is shares into two classes. Those shares with the GOOGL symbol retained all rights. A second set of shares with the GOOG symbol does not have shareholder voting rights. Sometimes, but not always, nonvoting shares can have a higher dividend payout than voting shares.

Stock Indexes

An index is a group of stocks whose values are pooled together using a mathematical formula. As each stock in the index trades, its most recent price is processed through the formula, leading to the value that is reported during the stock market trading day and when stocks stop trading at the close. An example of indexing is the frequent value quoting of the Dow Jones Industrial Average, the most commonly quoted stock index in the world. A Dow quote of 16,000 means that it would cost $16,000 to buy one share of the index at that place in time.

Types of Stock Indexes

There are dozens of indexes that quantify the value of groups of stocks, but they can all be divided into two major categories: diversified and sector specific. Diversified indexes house several types of stocks, while sector specific indexes measure the value of stocks in the same sector of the economy.

The Dow Jones Industrial Average (the Dow) is composed of thirty large global blue chips, or high-quality corporations in different industries. Members of the Dow Jones Industrial Average include software giant Microsoft and oil behemoth ExxonMobil. The Standard & Poor's 500 Index (S&P 500) has 500 large companies. It's considered "the" market benchmark because it has more stocks than the Dow; thus, it can provide a wider view of the market and how the market is reflecting economic activity.

The Nasdaq Composite Index (NASDAQ) has over 4,000 stocks. It's traditionally weighted toward technology companies, but is considered a diversified index as it also has biotech, banking, and energy stocks.

Sector specific indexes include the Semiconductor Index (SOX), the Biotech Index (BTK), and the Bank Index (BKX). Each of these sector indexes contains only the stocks in that particular sector of the economy. For example, SOX includes Intel and companies that are involved in the semiconductor chip sector. You can find companies like Amgen in BTK. And banks like J.P. Morgan, Chase, and Bank of America are pooled into the Bank Index.

ALERT

It's a good idea to become familiar with both sector and diversified indexes as you progress in your investment activity because the action in any particular sector of the market can have a significant effect on the "whole" market, which means that if you own a diversified mutual fund, but the banking stocks are being sold, your mutual fund may drop in value.

Types of Stocks

There are two broad categories of stocks: those that provide growth and those that provide income in the form of dividends. Growth refers to a company's ability to grow its sales, revenues, and eventually, earnings. Growth companies offer investors the opportunity for capital appreciation. In this case, you make money by buying low and selling high. Generally speaking, growth stocks are companies in their early stages of being publically traded. As the company matures, growth tends to slow and the stocks start paying dividends, which produce income. Profits produce dividends. Income stocks are primarily owned for their dividend payouts.

FACT

Dividends are portions of a company's profits that are passed on to shareholders. They are usually, but not always, paid out on a quarterly basis. Some companies pay a quarterly dividend but also pay out extra dividends throughout the year depending on individual situations. You can get a great deal of information on dividends at a great website: *www.dividend.com.*

Inside Growth Stocks

A pure growth company was Tesla Motors, Inc. in its early days. It paid no dividends, but its price rose dramatically for an extended period of time after its initial public offering based on the expectations of investors for the company to grow its business.

Two good examples of growth companies that followed the transition from pure growth to dividend payers are Starbucks and Google. Both are strong companies that will continue to grow. But because their growth rates slowed after their first decade or so of being publically traded, and because their ability to make money was well established, they began paying dividends.

The Income Producers

Income stocks are also known as "yield" stocks. These stocks tend to be those of older, established companies that pay out a high percentage of their earnings to shareholders through dividends. The most common yield stocks are those of electric utility companies. Blue chip oil stocks, like ExxonMobil and tobacco giant Altria Group, are also reliable dividend payers. Altria's dividend is very popular, and it attracts buyers to the stock. It's a rare hybrid investment as it pays a great dividend and offers the opportunity for price appreciation. It's a good idea to own both growth stocks and dividend-paying stocks in any diversified portfolio.

A special kind of dividend-paying stock is the preferred stock. This type of stock pays a higher yield than the common stock of a company and has a lifespan defined by its redemption date. It also pays a guaranteed fixed dividend that gets paid no matter what the company's earnings do.

Preferred stocks are always part of a class of shares, determined by the company when the stock is issued to the public. If XYZ has both common and preferred shares, XYZ common has the symbol XYZ when it trades. Its preferred stocks trade as XYZ.A, XYZ.B, and so on, depending on how many classes of preferred stocks there may be. Aside from paying a higher dividend yield, preferred stock holders have no vote at the annual company meeting and do not have any of the rights of holders of common shares. That means that if you don't like what a company is doing, when it comes time to vote for change, you are out of the loop. That's the price for getting a higher dividend.

ALERT

Beware of dividend-paying stocks with an extraordinarily high yield, or dividend rate. If either a common or a preferred stock has an uncommonly high dividend yield, especially compared to similar companies in its sector, or the overall market, as measured by the S&P 500, there is usually a reason to be careful. High dividends are often a sign that the stock price has fallen significantly and that the company has not cut its dividend. That is usually a sign that the company is in trouble. A good rule of thumb is to check the dividend yield of the S&P 500 online at *www.multpl.com/s-p-500-dividend-yield* and use it for comparison. For example, if the S&P 500 yield is 2% and XYZ common is paying 8%, you need to do more research before chasing that high dividend.

General Characteristics of Growth Versus Income

Growth stocks can be very risky. They tend to be the section of the market where day traders and momentum traders make their living. These stocks can move, up or down, in a big way in a short period of time. By the same token, you can also reap a larger reward by taking the risks of owning some growth stocks. One way to cut risks is to own a growth stock mutual fund that owns large numbers of growth stocks and can cushion the risk of one or two stocks that happen to have a big move to the downside on any given day.

ALERT

Fast-moving growth stocks are also known as momentum stocks. Momentum stocks tend to rally over long periods of time and make huge gains over the period. Eventually they all come crashing down. Beware, not even these go-go stocks go up forever.

Sizing Up Individual Stocks

There are three capitalization categories in the stock market: small, midsize, and large. Capitalization is the worth of the company in the public market. To calculate any stock's market capitalization you multiply the current price of the stock by the number of outstanding shares.

Small and midsize stocks are also known as small-cap and mid-cap. These are companies whose market capitalization, or value, is less than $2 billion for small and between $1 billion and $5 billion for mid-cap. Anything above $5 billion is considered large-cap. Blue chip stocks are those with very large market values, such as Apple Inc., Microsoft, and Google. Some stocks skip going from small- to large-cap. For example Facebook debuted as a blue chip capitalization stock with a market value of over $100 billion on its IPO.

The definition of market capitalization tends to shift based on whether the market is trading at a very high or low level. For example, if the market has been declining for a long time, the definition of a small-cap stock might differ from what it would be if the market happened to be trading near its all-time highs. In a declining market, small-cap may be defined as stocks with market caps at $1 billion or less, while large-cap may refer to stocks that are valued over $3 billion. The take-home message is that there are several tiers of stocks and that each tier has its own characteristics.

Google's market cap at the close of trading on April 3, 2014, was 383.6 billion. Stock quotes at *www.finance.yahoo.com* automatically provide stock market capitalization values.

Small-Cap Stocks

Smaller stocks tend to be faster growers, but they may be small for a good reason, such as their products are very niche-specific or because they are a development stage company and don't have any products in the market. Many speculative biotechnology stocks are in the small-cap sector. As a class, small stocks tend to be riskier than large-cap stocks. They usually don't pay dividends. By the same token, a small company, which is able to expand its sales, earnings, and scope, may become a mid-cap, a large-cap, or a blue chip stock at some point in the future. As with growth stocks, owning a well-managed, well-established small-cap stock mutual fund can help to reduce the risk of owning these individual companies. The benchmark index for small-cap stocks is the Russell 2000 Index (RUT) of small-cap stocks.

Mid-Cap Stocks: The Sweet Spot in the Market

Because they are usually well-established companies that have a track record, have stable earnings, often pay dividends, and tend to grow rapidly, mid-cap stocks are often referred to as the sweet spot of the market. Don't let that fool you, though. As with any area of the market, mid-cap stocks can be risky; therefore, doing your homework is essential in this area of the market as well. The benchmark index for mid-cap stocks is the Standard & Poor's MidCap 400 Index (MID). As with other areas and sectors of the market, a mid-cap stock mutual fund is worth considering.

Blue Chip and Large-Cap Stocks

Blue chip stocks are the names everyone recognizes when they think of the stock market. These are companies like Walmart, Procter & Gamble, and Pfizer. The Dow Jones Industrial Average houses thirty of the bluest of blue chip stocks in the world. But the S&P 500 also has its share of blue chip stocks, as well as being the home of the 500 largest stocks in the U.S. stock market. Blue chip stocks are usually near the top of their industry, deliver reasonably predictable earnings on a quarterly basis, and are often the backbone of conservative stock portfolios. Large numbers of mutual funds and institutional investors own blue chip stocks.

Cyclical, Defensive, and Value Stocks

Three other categories of stocks that you should be aware of are cyclical, defensive, and value stocks. These categories describe small-cap, mid-cap, large-cap, and blue chip stocks that behave in particular ways.

Cyclical stocks are companies whose price action tends to shift with the business cycle. These include the steel, chemical, construction, heavy machinery, and mining companies. Generally, when the economy is expanding, these stocks tend to move higher. A great example of a cyclical stock is Dow Chemical (NYSE: DOW). These stocks can be difficult to buy and hold for short periods of time, but can be important parts of long-term holdings because they often pay very good dividends.

Defensive stocks tend to be relatively stable and often have very small price fluctuations. This category includes utility and health care stocks. They are not immune from long-term down trends in the market, but they tend to hold their value better during down periods than most growth and momentum stocks.

ALERT

When looking at any stock, whether it's a growth, cyclical, defensive, or value candidate, consider where the market is at any one time. For example, if the overall market, as measured by the S&P 500, has rallied 5%–8% or more in a few weeks, it's a good idea to wait before you buy. Those kinds of gains by the market are usually followed by some kind of pullback. It's better to buy stocks when prices have fallen some and are starting to show signs of stabilizing.

Value stocks are those that are cheap relative to the overall value of the market. These are usually stocks of companies that are doing quite well but are being ignored by the market, which tends to focus on momentum stocks a fair amount of the time. Value investors tend to be very patient and often have to wait for long periods of time before the market recognizes their stock. Value stocks tend to be companies that sell at less than two times their book value. As of April 2014, Goldman Sachs (NYSE: GS) was selling at 1.11 times its book value. This was a classic value scenario.

Important Market Sectors

The S&P 500 is divided into ten sectors. Each sector is given a weighting in the index, which is the amount of influence it has on the overall price of the index. As of April 2014, these were the weightings:

- Information Technology: 18.6%
- Financials: 16.4%
- Health Care: 13.3%
- Consumer Discretionary: 12.1%
- Industrials: 10.6%
- Energy: 10.2%
- Consumer Staples: 9.7%
- Materials: 3.5%
- Utilities: 3.1%
- Telecom Services: 2.5%

You can see that the "sexy" sectors are the most influential, with Information Technology, Financials, and Health Care adding up to nearly 50% of the index. If you were to construct your own S&P index–inspired stock portfolio, this is the model that you would use. This weighting changes over time depending on the economy and the general state of the markets, but the top three categories in this list are consistently near the top as they reflect the dominant sectors of the U.S. economy.

Penny Stocks

When you go to any news websites, you'll see the ads that promise millions of dollars through penny stocks. If some fast-talking guy from New Jersey calls you out of the blue to pitch the new Apple to you, don't believe him. Penny stocks are almost always a sure way to lose money. Yes, you'll read about how Apple and Microsoft were once penny stocks. Consider that Google, Facebook, and Twitter were not penny stocks when they went public. So the odds of those kinds of success stories repeating are almost zero.

Penny stocks are stocks with a price generally below $5 per share. And there is usually a good reason for it, such as the company is losing money, doesn't have any viable products, or has fallen on hard times. Does that mean that it may not be a good opportunity? Not necessarily. It just means that you should be careful. Unscrupulous brokers who call you and tell you that they have the next Microsoft for one dollar a share are often scam artists who work in a "boiler room," a big phone bank pushing fraudulent shares of stocks.

If you decide to take a chance on penny stocks, do your homework. Research the company, its products, and its management team. Consider their business sector and their competition. If they actually do have the new "Holy Grail" and no one but you has figured it out, you may actually defy the odds and hit that one in a million home run. But don't bet on it too much. Invest small amounts, and pay attention to news and the general state of the business.

CHAPTER 5

Choosing Stocks to Buy

The ideal stock is one that moves steadily higher, pays a good dividend, and has all the characteristics of a great company. Keep in mind, though, that evaluating and buying stocks is no easy matter. After all, you are putting real money into a financial instrument whose price rises and falls, often several times within a few minutes. That means that in order to be a successful stock investor, you need careful thought and a well-put-together plan that lets you pick winners consistently and lets you know when it's time to sell.

Five Points That Make a Great Company

There are five characteristics of a great company:

1. Great products and an iconic brand
2. Superb management
3. Excellent customer service
4. Adaptability to current trends and changes in current customer needs
5. Accountability to shareholders

In other words, a great company has great products, great corporate ethics, excellent management, and is able to communicate its sucesses as well as its failures in a timely and honest fashion. A terrible company is usually marked by shifty management, inconsistent returns, and a lack of direction.

Analyzing Starbucks

Starbucks is a perfect example of a great company because it meets all of the criteria and excels in the way it runs its business while maintaining a socially conscious focus as a bonus.

Starbucks began in 1971 in Seattle, Washington. Currently, the company has over 19,000 retail stores in over sixty countries.

Great Products and an Iconic Brand

Imagine going somewhere and not seeing a Starbucks logo. It's hard, right? Being all over the place is what is known as an indelible and ubiquitous presence. And this is what great companies do best. They become part of the social fabric. They become a part of people's lives and a part of the visual landscape that can't be easily erased. By being everywhere and delivering excellent products consistently, great companies make money on a consistent basis. Starbucks's coffee and related products are always of the highest quality. Because of this, the company can charge a premium for its products, a fact that adds to its profit margins and bottom line. This, in turn, leads to a greater tendency of the stock price to rise.

Management

Starbucks's management team is top-notch. Chairman Howard Schultz understands the business of coffee, but also understands the needs of the company's multiple constituents. He is very articulate in announcing and promoting the company's strategies and is conscientious about monitoring progress, maintaining company operations, and communicating with customers, suppliers, and shareholders.

Customer Service

The company's customer service is top-notch as the front-line baristas deliver the drinks ordered by customers with accuracy and good attitude. This is part of the company's culture and starts in the boardroom, working its way down. Starbucks shops are clean and comfortable and offer excellent amenities, such as Wi-Fi, comfortable lounging chairs and sofas, and tasteful background music. These are factors that encourage customers to hang around the shop and maybe order more drinks.

Adaptability and Innovation

Companies have to remain relevant in order to maintain and grow revenues and earnings. Starbucks not only adapts to current trends by varying its menu options, but it often sets new trends by introducing new products and expanding its accessory lines, such as company-branded coffeemakers and high-end cups, mugs, and gift packages, at its stores. A great example of innovation is the way that the company's products are promoted. Take Starbucks gift cards. These little bits of plastic with prepaid purchases attached are among the most popular tokens of appreciation given by friends to one another and are also used by employers to reward employees.

Having a great variety of products adds to the mix. Starbucks offers health-conscious fare, such as fruit and protein plates, but also has what it calls "indulgent" treats, such as scones and apple fritters. It lets weight-conscious customers order drinks with variable ingredients such as low-calorie sweeteners and skim milk.

Consistency is key to a great company. Starbucks excels at this because their offerings are always consistent. You can go to a Starbucks in Seattle or Boston, and your drink will taste the same in both shops.

The company also innovates and makes timely changes in its product lines and is often the first to strike in a new category. For example, it offers new flavors of lattes and new food choices on a regular basis while maintaining a good balance with products that are customer favorites. It saw an opportunity to expand its corporate line and made a distribution deal with Green Mountain (Nasdaq: GMCR), a competitor, in order to enter a sector where it was lagging. And it diversifies its offerings with juices, bottled water, and music CDs.

Accountability to Shareholders

Aside from having great products and running a profitable company that is tuned in to customer needs, a great company has to take care of its shareholders. You don't want to buy stock in a company that does not have the shareholders' best interests in mind. That's where listening in on company earnings calls, reading press, and keeping up with media and analyst coverage of the company pays off. Starbucks's press releases and earnings calls are usually frank and truthful and contain useful information. If you can't listen to the calls, they will have transcripts of the calls on their website. Starbucks rarely sugarcoats its future expectations and tends to admit when it's made a strategic mistake while offering solutions. It's not perfect, but it's a good model to use for comparison when defining the "Great Company."

Buy What You Know and Know What You Buy

As simple as this concept sounds, it's a great place to start when you are looking to jump-start your stock picking. You use health products on a regular basis. You travel; you buy groceries; you stay at hotels; you have a bank; and you can see what other people are eating or driving, and what credit cards they use most often. You also know that even though a product is popular, it may be a fleeting phenomenon, which is why your personal knowledge of a concept or a product is a great place to start, but not the only factor that you should use in deciding whether to buy a stock.

Once you've picked a product and decided on a company, consider these factors:

- Does this company meet the criteria of a great company?
- What is the current sales growth and momentum?
- What is the current earnings growth and momentum?
- How is the valuation?
- How is this stock behaving compared to the market?
- Does this company pay dividends and is it growing?

Is This a Great Company?

This is an easy one. Let's say that you just bought a new cell phone from a startup company that is trying to expand its market share (XYZ). You like the phone and you start seeing other people buying it. That's the signal that more work is in order. That's when you apply the "Five Point" approach to the "Great Company." Check the five points:

- Great products
- Management
- Customer service
- Adaptability and innovation
- Accountability to shareholders

See what the answers are. If the company earns the five points that describe a great company, it's time to do more homework.

Checking Sales and Momentum

Sales come from selling cell phones and accessories. A good rule of thumb for growth companies is that they should have at least three or more quarters of sales growth. You want to see more than 20% and you want to see it accelerating. Those are the companies that hit the home runs. Sales momentum, or the ability to continue to grow sales, is hugely important, especially when evaluating growth stocks. If sales rates are stuck or decreasing, but you still see more XYZ phones around, it may be worth it to keep an eye on the company and see what it does over the next couple of quarters. You may be catching it at a period when the sales growth has not been reported. In this case, considering a very small position, especially if the stock is rising in price, could make sense.

ALERT

A perfect example of how sales growth can affect stocks is the Apple iPhone versus BlackBerry dynamic. As Apple's phone shares accelerated, BlackBerry shares began to decline. This was evident by the number of people who were switching from BlackBerry to Apple phones. As a result, Apple stock soared while BlackBerry fell to near penny stock territory. When Android phones became more visible and popular, Apple shares started to falter.

Earnings and Revenue Growth

Revenue is the amount of money that a company collects on its sales. Revenue growth means that a company is not just selling product, but it is able to collect on what it sells. That's a sign that it's selling products to sound customers. Earnings are also known as the bottom line. This is what's left over after a company pays its bills.

Ideally, you want to see earnings and revenues grow simultaneously. If revenues are growing faster than earnings, the company may have a lot of debt and may not deliver earnings for some time. This is acceptable for young companies but not for established companies. You want both a strong top- and bottom-line growth rate. Ten percent or above is excellent and is sustainable. When revenues and earnings start to falter, it could be a sign that harder times are ahead and that evaluating whether you want to hold on to the stock makes sense.

Valuation

Valuation describes whether a stock is cheap or expensive. There are many ways to express valuation, but price to book and price/earnings ratio are simple, accurate, and easy to find as part of stock quote information at stock market websites such as *www.marketwatch.com* and *www.bloomberg.com*.

Price/earnings (P/E) ratio describes how much you are paying for every dollar of earnings. To calculate a P/E ratio, you divide the price of the stock by the most recent earnings per share. A price/earnings ratio of 10 is considered "normal" while a P/E ratio above 20 is generally considered expensive. There are some subtleties to consider. For example, it's not uncommon to see P/E ratios in the high teens for growth stocks. Facebook's P/E ratio in early April, 2014, was 93. Investors were expecting Facebook's earnings growth to continue and were willing to pay for it. By comparison, Google's P/E during the same period was nearly 14. At that valuation, Google was acting more like a value stock than a growth stock, although it was still growing and expanding its commercial reach.

Price to book refers to the relationship between the price of the stock and the book value, the value of all of the company's assets. Comparing Google's price to book (4.31) to Facebook's (9) you can see that the lower the value of the price to book, the cheaper the stock is.

ESSENTIAL

Look at the whole picture. If you have doubts, compare Google, a monster company that sells at 14 times earnings and 4 times book value while basically owning the search engine market in the world, to Facebook, a growing company selling at an inflated P/E and price to book ratio. In a strong momentum market, owning Facebook may make sense. In a less stable market, it may make sense to own Google.

Price to book value can be misleading. Some company shares sell below book value and may not be cheap. In fact, they may be failing. Their earnings and revenues may be sinking rapidly, and the only thing they have left could be bankruptcy and sale of assets. It's the assets, such as buildings and other things that the company may own, that give it any value at all. Valuation, thus, is only a small part of the overall analytical survey that you should consider.

Relative Strength

Relative strength (RS) is a measure of how a stock performs in comparison to the market. The most common comparison is between an individual stock and the S&P 500. The higher the number, the better, as it means that your stock's price is rising faster than that of the whole index. When this happens, relative strength is considered positive. A back of the napkin method of calculating this metric is as follows: If XYZ stock is trading at 50 and the S&P 500 is trading at 1800, divide 50 by 1800. XYZ's relative strength is 0.027. You can graph this on a daily or weekly basis if you're a stickler for details and spreadsheets. Investors.com (*www.investors.com*) displays the daily RS for all the stocks it lists in its daily stock quotes.

As with any other aspect of stock analysis, you need to put relative strength in the proper perspective. If you own a bank stock that pays a steady dividend and the stock is rising at half the rate of the S&P 500, you are not necessarily in a bad position. Your stock is rising and you are getting dividends. On the other hand, if you own a growth stock and its relative strength is fading, it's likely a sign that you may have to consider selling it.

Dividends

Dividends are important, but they are not everything. Think of them as getting rent for being patient with a stock that is not moving very much. By the same token, avoid stocks that are either falling or not holding their value. If a dividend isn't enough to keep stockholders in the stock, something must be going on behind the scenes. When stocks don't behave well, it's often because there are rumors that a management shakeup is looming or that a large investor may know something that the market will learn in the future and he or she is getting out while the getting is good. Dividends, then, should be looked at within the context of how a company is doing, how it's running its business, and how it's managing its future.

To learn how good a stock dividend is, compare it to the following three benchmarks:

- The yield of the Ten-Year U.S. Treasury Note
- The dividend yield of the S&P 500
- The dividend yield of other stocks in its sector

Altria Group (NYSE:MO), the tobacco stock, has been a historical leader in dividends to its stockholders. In April 2014, the company's dividend yield was 5%. In comparison, the Ten-Year U.S. Treasury Note was paying nearly 2.7% and the S&P 500's dividend yield was 2.05%. Dividend yields for other stocks in the tobacco group included 4.54% for Philip Morris (NYSE: PM). In this case, from purely a dividend-paying standpoint, Altria was the best bet. That's the first step. Next, you would put your "Five Point" method to work.

Know Where You Are in the Market Cycle

The most difficult part of investing in stocks is knowing when it's best to buy, hold, or sell. If you don't pay attention to this bit of timing, you could end up losing large sums of money, and sometimes in a hurry.

Bull Versus Bear Market

A bull market is a stock market in which prices are rising. A bear market is the opposite. In a bull market, the odds of picking stock winners is significantly higher than of doing so in a bear market, where the predominant direction of prices is down. What this means is that investing with the overall trend in stocks is your best bet to make money.

Being a Contrarian: Know When to Buck the Trend

A contrarian is an investor who can spot the time when it makes sense to go against the predominant price trend. For example, contrarians tend to buy near the market bottoms and sell near market tops. That's because they know that, generally speaking, a bull market starts when most people are expecting that stocks will never rise again. During recessions, the economy is declining and companies are making less money. Thus, their stock prices fall as investors realize that profits and earnings will fall as a result of the troubled economy.

Usually, as a response to hard economic times, the Federal Reserve lowers interest rates aggressively and eventually stock prices start to rise as lower interest rates decrease the return of savings accounts and other interest-paying instruments. At some point, the economy usually improves, at least enough for stock prices to justify their gains, and more investors come in, fueling higher prices.

ALERT

Bull markets are hard charging. Stock prices rise on a frequent basis, the economy is usually steady, and the outlook for profits is positive. During bear markets, the opposite is true. A bear market takes a bite out of your portfolio and puts fear into the markets. Prices are falling, the economy is weak, and the profit outlook is uncertain.

A bear market is the opposite. These are nasty periods when stock prices fall, usually for long periods of time, often years. Bear markets result from either too much speculation in stocks, when the Federal Reserve raises interest rates, or both. In 2007 and 2008, stocks rolled over after the housing bubble burst. Prices fell throughout the year with almost no respite. This bear market corresponded to the economic period known as the Great Recession, and it began when too many people who bought homes on credit stopped making their mortgage payments. The banking system froze and the selling in stocks followed.

From October 2007 to March 2009, the S&P 500 lost nearly 57% of its value. In March 2009 when the market finally bottomed, as the Federal Reserve made it clear that interest rates would remain near zero for a very long time, stocks began a rally that as of March 2014 had gained nearly 180%. If you had tried to buy stocks as the market was falling in 2007 through 2009, you would have had little luck. If you tried to sell stocks in the five years that followed, you would have sold too early. Never forget this. Before you invest, make sure that the market is giving you good odds of being successful in your stock picks. Here is a three-point checklist that will keep you safe when analyzing the market:

- Know whether stocks have been rising for a short or a long period of time. The longer the time that prices have been rising, the higher the odds of a significant decline.
- Know what the Federal Reserve plans to do with interest rates in the short and long term. Lower interest rates favor stocks. Higher interest rates eventually lead to lower stock prices. In March 2014, the Federal Reserve hinted that they would raise interest rates by the middle of 2015 and stocks began to falter.
- Understand that even though you may buy the stock of a solid company, if the market reverses its trend and falls into a bear market or a significant correction in prices, your stock will likely fall along with the majority of stocks.

Technical Analysis: The Art of Reading Price Charts

Technical analysis refers to the study of price charts. Price patterns tend to repeat themselves and similar events tend to precede or follow similar price patterns. This can be true at important market bottoms (such as March 2009) and significant market tops (such as October 2007). Technical analysis works best when it is used with fundamental analysis, such as getting to know your companies and studying their valuation.

There are entire and very thorough books dedicated to technical analysis that you can find by going to *www.amazon.com* or your local bookstore. And there are some great websites that are worth getting familiar with. One is *www.stockcharts.com*. StockCharts.com offers a great deal of free content and lets you customize charts in a way that is easy for you to understand. It also has great basic information and offers tutorials, which will help you learn how to read and analyze price charts and get comfortable with chart analysis.

CHAPTER 6

Buying Stocks and Monitoring Progress

This chapter is all about giving you information that will help you make the transition from paper investor to real-life stock picker. It starts with methods that offer you support and progresses toward the point where you can fly on your own. After reading you can decide which way to go based on your own risk tolerance and personality.

Investment Clubs

A nice transition from paper investing to real-life investing can be made through investment clubs. This is where a group of friends form a partnership and pool their money, and each member performs a certain function, whether it is analyzing a sector of the market or individual stocks of a certain category. The average club meets about once a month, has a good discussion about the potential stocks that they might buy, monitors any existing holdings, and then votes on their next course of action. Clubs tend to work better when members agree on a stock-picking philosophy, but members should be open to new ideas and often invite outside guest speakers for educational opportunities.

A nonprofit organization called BetterInvesting (*www.betterinvesting.org*) has been around for decades and is a great resource for investment clubs. BetterInvesting takes you from zero to being a fully operational club via its online tutorials, educational materials, and blogs. *BetterInvesting* magazine has timely educational articles that continue the education process. BetterInvesting charges a fee for registering the club and charges individual members a fee as well.

ESSENTIAL

The advantage of an investment club is that you can share the work and the reward. You also spread the risk of any potential losses and can learn from the experience of more than one person. When things don't go so well, an investment club offers the advantage of having someone with which to share the misery and the comfort food.

Most investment clubs tend to focus on long-term investment strategies that involve owning growth stocks and require that members contribute to periodic investments into the markets. Clubs tend to reinvest dividends and use a technique called dollar cost averaging, which involves putting a fixed amount of money to work at a predetermined interval, such as every two months. When stock prices drop, dollar cost averaging allows for buying larger quantities of shares. Rising prices will lead to lower numbers of shares using this technique.

Dividend Reinvestment Plans (DRIPs)

Another way to slowly dip your toes in the water, and a nice complement to an investment club, is a dividend reinvestment plan. These plans let you buy shares of common stock directly from the company. In most cases, you have to own at least one share of stock in the company through a broker before you can join the DRIP. There may be a handling fee to the company for keeping your shares, but there is no broker commission. This is a great vehicle for buying shares of stock with low costs and is tailor-made for companies that pay dividends. You build up your position over time by buying shares at regular intervals and reinvesting the dividends. Reinvested dividends buy shares, or partial shares, of stock. If your stock sells for $100 and your dividend is $25, it would buy you one fourth of a share.

DRIP investing isn't for everyone. However, when you are starting out, it makes sense to at least look into it. You can find a good amount of information, articles, calculators, and even DRIP investing candidates at The DRIP Investment Resource Center, *www.dripinvesting.org*.

Who Will Do the Investing?

Once you've decided that you are going to be investing in stocks, you need to figure out how you will buy and sell your shares. There are two important questions to answer:

Who will make the buy and sell decisions, and will you use a full commission or a discount broker to build and manage your portfolio?

Traditional Full-Service Brokers

A traditional full-service broker is a professional who is in an office, has a book of clients, and uses research produced by the company she works for to pick stocks, which she then recommends to her client. She may have a large number of clients and may or may not do much in the way of making judgments about you as an individual investor. Traditional brokers pass licensure exams and are registered investment advisors. They charge fairly large commissions and may also charge retainer fees for managing your portfolio. Traditional brokers get paid whether you make or lose money. Depending on your contractual agreement with your broker, she may have full discretion or partial discretion to trade your account. Full-service brokers and advisors tend to market their services toward wealthy clients, so finding one who is conscientious about small accounts can be a difficult task.

ALERT

Beware a full-service broker or advisor who only markets financial instruments sold by her company. These products, such as mutual funds and annuities, can have hefty fees and can often charge you even larger fees if you change your mind and want to exit them before a certain period of time.

Discount Brokers

Discount brokers usually have branch offices as well as an online presence. The very large discount brokers such as Fidelity Investments (*www.fidelity.com*) and Scottrade (*www.scottrade.com*) have excellent and comfortable branch offices where you can conduct business. These branch offices have computer terminals for research and trading, product brochures, and representatives to assist you. The representatives can answer questions, help you fill out forms, make exchanges between mutual funds, process withdrawals and deposits from your accounts, and set up appointments with investment advisors. Discount brokers also offer managed accounts and financial planning options for additional costs.

Online discount brokers offer the following advantages:

- **Control.** You can make decisions on your own schedule and make decisions based on your own experience and research. You can trade when you are ready instead of waiting for your broker to call you back.
- **Convenience.** With an online brokerage account you have access to your financial information at the speed of light from anywhere on your computer, laptop, or mobile phone. You can even make portfolio decisions while you are on vacation. If the market goes against you or your stock hits a sell point, you can do it in seconds from anywhere. If you need to

interact with someone, discount brokers offer toll-free phone access and branch offices.

- **Efficiency.** Because of intense competition, online brokers are much cheaper than full-service traditional brokers. Online discount brokers where you make your own decisions, in many cases, charge less than $10 for executing your trades. Compare this to full-service brokers where you may get some hand holding and access to research that is disseminated to thousands of clients for several times the same amount of money.

The DIY Investor

If you decide to go about investing by yourself, you will have to put some work into it. It's not that difficult, but it does require effort. You have to do your own research and make your own decisions. Aside from buying stock in companies that you may be familiar with, it's also important to figure out the market's prevalent trend, look for strong sectors, and consider which stocks, if any, in that sector make sense to buy after you apply your analysis system, including the "Five Points" that make a great company.

DIY investors usually fare better with online brokers. Commissions are lower and most offer excellent support systems, including access to charts and to company fundamental information.

Consider a Consultant Advisor

It may make sense to get a second opinion when faced with a difficult decision. In those cases, it's good to find an advisor who may charge an hourly fee for providing an opinion on your portfolio. This may be a financial planner, your CPA, a registered investment advisor, or even a broker who consults with individuals who like to make their own investment decisions.

Your Buy List

Once you've set up your account, it's time to put together your buy list. Here is where you put together what you know and what you've learned so far. First, consider whether you are in a bull or bear market. If stocks are generally moving higher, it's the former. If the economy is in bad shape, it's very likely that stocks are by and large falling. Either way, there is no harm in putting together a buy list.

Know Your Symbols

One of the first things you need to do to familiarize yourself with how the stock market operates is to learn the abbreviated names of stocks, known as stock symbols. The New York Stock Exchange usually tags stocks with three-letter names, while the Nasdaq uses four letters. There are exceptions. Facebook (Nasdaq: FB) is only two letters on the Nasdaq, while Twitter (NYSE: TWTR) is an example of a four-letter symbol on the New York Stock Exchange. Online financial websites include the name of the stock and the symbol when they mention the company in articles. The references are linked to charts and news items.

Use the Stock Tables

Traditional stock tables, such as those found in newspapers, also list the name and the symbol. One of the most comprehensive stock table listings is in *Barron's* magazine (*www.barrons.com*). Stock tables also include useful information, such as the high and low price over the last fifty-two weeks, the price/earnings ratio, dividends paid, dividend yield, the recent closing price, and the net change from the previous day's trading.

Putting Your List Together

You can start with as many stocks as you like and then pare your list down to the best of the bunch. Include the stocks of the companies whose products you use. Most consumer product companies pay reliable dividends. Consult the daily "New Highs" list that you can find on financial websites such as that of the *Wall Street Journal* (*www.wsj.com*) and Investors.com (*www.investors.com*). These are usually high growth stocks. Include some value, growth, and income stocks in your list and pick a few of each to include. Buy small numbers of shares, initially. You can add larger numbers later.

Don't have more stocks in your portfolio than you can keep up with. For a beginning investor, owning any more than ten stocks at any one time is probably too many. A good way to progress in your ability to pick stocks and to manage a diversified portfolio is by learning the steps through participating in your investment club. Once you get the hang of it you can start venturing out on your own.

ESSENTIAL

Don't be in a hurry to start investing. It's better to take baby steps over a few months to a couple of years than to become overwhelmed and discouraged by trying to do too much too soon. Learn as much as you can about where your money will be going before you take the plunge.

Think about Your Time Frame and Risk Tolerance

For most people, investing is a long-term process where they are looking for profits months or years after they buy a stock. That means that they are willing to be patient and will allow larger price fluctuations before making large changes to their portfolio. Long-term investors often see a price drop as an opportunity to buy more shares at a cheaper price, as long as they are comfortable with the long-term prospects of the company.

If you are a nervous and impatient person, you definitely want to study short-term trading techniques and become familiar with charting and technical analysis in fairly good detail before you start buying and selling stocks. Before you delve into trading, consider that you can lose a great deal of money rapidly even if you are experienced.

Know Your Exit Point Before You Buy

Whether you are a patient long-term investor or a rapid-fire day trader, it's best to know your exit point before you buy a stock. There are two ways of doing this. Long-term investors often set targets, both in terms of price and time. You may decide that you will need the money in XYZ shares five years from the day you buy it, and you manage the position according to that strategy.

If you buy a stock and your goal is to make a certain amount of money, it becomes more difficult to achieve your exit point. You must remain vigilant.

If you follow this price targeting strategy, you may buy a stock at $50 and set a target to sell it at $60. That price may be reached in three months or two years. If the stock hits the sell point in a short period of time, you can sell some of your shares since they hit your exit point, and let the rest of the position remain open and continue to move higher.

If you choose to let the partial open position ride, you can set another target and repeat the strategy. If you choose the second scenario, you should remember that your original target price was $60. If the stock rallies for a short period after it hits $60 and then rolls over and moves lower, you should stick to your target and sell it at $60 on the way back down. Short-term trading involves cutting losses at a certain percentage if a stock goes the wrong way. This is known as a sell-stop. You can set sell-stops either in terms of price points or in terms of percentages after you buy shares.

Executing Stock Trades

When you're ready to start trading, your number one concern is how to execute your trades. If you use a full-service broker, you would do that with a phone call. If you use an online discount broker, then you'll be using your mouse. When you call your broker, you wait until your order is confirmed. When you trade online, you just follow the menu instructions, point and click, and your confirmation is on the screen almost immediately. Become familiar with the several types of buy and sell orders, and consider which one fits your strategy best before you actually trade. As a beginning investor, you may be best served by using market orders and considering the use of a sell stop. As you gain more experience you can consider more specific order types.

Market Orders

This is the most common order used by individual investors. It means you want to buy or sell stocks at the current market price, or the going rate. Your order will be executed at the prevailing price when it hits the trading floor or the market maker. You will see two prices quoted, bid (the buy price) and ask (the sell price). The difference between the two prices is the spread. An example of Apple shares' bid price may be 522.57, while the ask price may be 522.90. The spread is 0.33. Market makers and floor traders, also known as dealers, are the middlemen in the transaction. They keep a large portion of the spread as commission for taking the other side of the trade with you.

Stock prices are now listed in digital notation compared to fraction quotes that were used in the past. This is a fairly small spread because Apple is a very liquid stock, meaning that there are lots of buyers and sellers. The price that you get for a stock may be different than the bid and ask, especially in stocks like Apple, where the price changes quickly.

Less liquid stocks, stocks that trade less frequently, may have wider spreads. The closer the spread, the better your price is likely to be. Low volume stocks can be difficult to buy but are usually more difficult to sell at a price that is favorable, especially if you have a small number of shares.

Limit Orders

Limit orders are used when you don't want to buy a stock for more or sell a stock for less than a predetermined price. Limit orders can be placed as day orders or good until canceled (GTC) orders. GTC orders have a better chance of being filled since day orders expire at the end of the trading day in which you place them.

Limit Order Buy

A limit order lets you attempt to buy a stock at a specific price. For example, if Apple is trading near $520 and you want to buy 100 shares only when the price falls to $515, you place a limit order for 100 shares of Apple at $515 per share. Your order may not get filled, as the stock may not fall to $515. It may also get filled at the first available lower price if the stock falls through $515. What you know is that your order will not get filled above $515.

Limit Order Sell

If you bought 100 shares of Apple at $515 and it climbs to $550, you might want to sell it at $555. By placing a limit sell order for 100 shares at $555, you know that your order will fill at least at $555. It may sell for a higher price, but it won't sell for less than $555.

Stop Order Sell

Stop orders to sell, also known as stop loss orders, are used to limit losses. If you bought Microsoft at $40 but you don't want to take a big loss if the stock starts to flounder, you can set a stop loss, in dollar amounts or in percentage amounts, below the price. For example, your stop order may be to sell 100 shares of Microsoft at $38. This limits your potential loss if the stock drops to $38 or below. Once your stock hits the stop point, it becomes a market order.

Stop Order Buy

Use stop orders to buy when you expect a stock to trade higher. If Microsoft is trading at $35 but is gathering steam, you may want to put in a stop order to buy 100 shares at $37. When the price hits $37, your order becomes a market order and may be filled above or below your stop price depending on market conditions.

Managing Your Money

At first, think in terms of dollar amounts, instead of number of shares. If you buy 100 shares of a $10 stock, it will cost you $1,000 plus commission. If you buy 10 shares of a $100 stock, it will cost you the same amount of money. If you have $10,000 and you want to own ten different company stocks, think about how you will divide the money among the ten stocks, and consider commission costs as well. If your commission is $7.95, and you buy ten different lots of stock, of varying share size, your commission will be $7.95 × 10 = $79.50 to buy and an equal amount if you were to sell them all at once.

It's a good idea to count every penny when you invest. When you're just starting out, you should work out your costs on paper before you actually make a trade. This will train you for the future, as you may progress into more complex, shorter term, trading strategies where money management is even more crucial.

Keeping Up with Your Stocks

Develop a monitoring routine based on your personality and your schedule. Checking your portfolio may be as easy as logging on to your online account periodically to see how things are going. The key is to be consistent and to be consciously involved. If you decide to check your portfolio every night, then do it every night. If you decide to check your portfolio once in the morning, once at lunch, and a third time an hour before the market closes on a daily basis, then that's your routine. The key is to figure out what works for you and then to be consistent.

When evaluating your portfolio's performance ask these questions:

- Are your investments keeping up with the market trend? This is especially important in rising markets where you want to see your stocks, ETFs, and mutual funds rise.
- Are your investments keeping up with your plan and your goals? This is especially important when you make your monthly or quarterly check. Compare your portfolio to both your goals and the market trend.
- Is it time to make changes? Have your goals changed? Is your portfolio not meeting your expectations? Should you talk to an advisor? These are all important aspects of portfolio management that should be part of your arsenal.

The Buyer's Checklist

There are many steps required in order to invest in stocks. Here is a recap of what you need to know in order to succeed:

- Start slowly by considering joining an investment club and using a dividend reinvestment plan.
- Decide on what kind of broker you will use.
- Develop a research routine.
- Put together a buy list.
- Know your goals and decide how you will sell a stock before you buy it.
- Understand the different kinds of orders to buy and sell your stocks.
- Manage your money and use this to balance your portfolio.
- Develop a portfolio management routine based on your risk profile and your schedule.
- Adjust your method as you become more experienced.

CHAPTER 7

Bonds: The Glue That Holds Financial Markets Together

To speak of bonds at a party is to seek loneliness. Yet, unknown to the masses, bonds are the real glue that holds the markets together. Think of it this way: Without bonds, the global economy would be a totally different place, one of much slower growth and fewer prospects. In this chapter you'll learn why bonds are important and how they make sense for your portfolio.

What Is a Bond?

A bond is a loan packaged as a marketable security. When investors buy bonds, they are loaning money to a company, a municipality, the federal government, or a foreign government with the expectation that the money will be paid back at a predetermined date in the future. Bonds pay interest, paid to the investor, in installments or as one lump sum when the bond matures. You can buy bonds directly as new issues from the government, company, or municipality, or you can buy them through traders, dealers, or brokers in the secondary market. The market sets bond prices as supply and demand changes.

The major reason investors buy bonds is usually the interest portion of the bond. In exchange for the loan, the issuer agrees to pay the investor interest at regular intervals as well as returning the original investment at maturity. Bonds are usually sold in discrete increments (multiples of $1,000). This is the par value or face value. Bond maturities are divided into short-, intermediate-, and long-term periods. Short-term bonds mature in less than five years. Intermediate-term bonds mature in five to ten years, while bonds with maturities above ten years are considered long-term. Bonds' maturities beyond twenty to thirty years are rare but do exist. Generally, bonds with the longer maturities pay the highest interest rates due to the higher risk potential. Bond prices and yields (the current effective interest rate) fluctuate based on any current market forces and trends. Rising prices lead to lower yields. This is important when you are trying to buy or sell bonds.

Bonds have a date of final maturity. That's when your initial investment, the principal, is returned. A callable bond is a special kind of bond that can be redeemed before the final maturity. If a bond is called, you get your money before the final maturity date. You still get your whole principal if the bond is called. You just don't collect the interest for as long as you expected. Most bonds pay interest semiannually or annually. The issuer has to inform investors whether a bond is callable before the sale. This information is part of the prospectus. If you are not sure ask the bond sales person about it before you buy.

ESSENTIAL

Bond prices often move in the opposite direction of stock prices. This is especially true of U.S. Treasury bonds, which are often seen as "safe" at times of market volatility or geopolitical tensions. This makes bonds an essential part of a diversified portfolio as rising bond prices can cushion any potential losses in stocks.

Why Do Bonds Rule the World?

While stocks get all the press and publicity, it's the hard-working bonds that pay the bills. Bonds allow governments, companies, and municipalities to finance projects sooner than they would be able to if they waited until they saved enough money to do so. So next time you see a big highway project, or a new factory being built, think about bonds as providing much if not all of the financial support.

Comparing Bonds Versus Stocks

A stock is a piece of a company. Stock investors, as partial owners, participate in the fortunes of the company. A bondholder is a lender. Lenders get paid unless the company goes bankrupt. This is why bonds are also known as fixed income investments. As a bondholder you know how much you will earn unless you sell the bond before maturity. For example: If you buy a one-year maturity $1,000 bond that pays 5%, you will receive $50 of interest in that year and you will receive your $1,000 back at maturity.

Corporate Versus Treasury Bonds

A U.S. Treasury bond is considered the safest bond in the world. That's because, even though the U.S. government pays its bills with borrowed money, it always pays its bills. That's why whenever there is major trouble in the world, such as a major war, or an economic crisis, investors flock to U.S. Treasury bonds. As they buy these bonds, prices rise and market interest rates drop.

Corporate bonds are different in that they often pay higher interest rates than treasury bonds but also offer higher risks. While the U.S. government has theoretically come close to a default on its bonds, as of April 2014, it has not defaulted. Corporations, on the other hand, have defaulted on their debt. This higher risk of default is the major difference between corporate and treasury bonds, and it's a major contributor to the higher interest rate usually paid by corporate bonds.

FACT

The U.S. government holds bond auctions on a regular basis. Some of the auctions are known as refunding auctions. Refunding auctions raise money for a specific purpose. That's when the government sells bonds and raises money to pay its interest debt to investors.

What Makes Bonds Risky?

Bonds are generally affected by particular factors that rarely affect stocks. The biggest risk is the risk of default, the possibility that you won't get paid. Inflation, the general state of the economy, credit risk, interest rate risk, and income risk are the others.

Credit Risk: Risk of Default

Although it's not very common, default does happen. When a company or government goes bankrupt, bondholders are first in line to collect on whatever is left after the legal haggling is done. But it often turns out that if there is anything to collect, it's a lot less than what you were expecting. In the post-2008 period, after the housing bubble burst, Greece defaulted on its debt, illustrating that government bonds are not exempt from default.

Bond ratings will be discussed later in this chapter. The major point is that bonds are assigned credit ratings by companies whose only function is to evaluate a bond's risk of default. As an investor, you must understand what credit ratings mean and how to make bond buying decisions based on these ratings.

Inflation and Economic Risk

Inflation is the enemy of fixed income investments. If you depend on the income from bonds, you lose money when prices of goods and services rise since your income can't grow as fast as inflation. This occurs even if your interest rate is higher than the rate of inflation. For example, if your bond pays 5% and inflation is growing at 3%, your net return is 2%. If inflation rises to 4%, your net return is now only 1%. This is the reason that bonds are good investments during periods of slow or falling economic growth. The only time this does not hold up is when inflation is rising during periods of slow economic growth. This is known as stagflation. If the economy is growing rapidly, it may be accompanied by inflation. If this is the scenario, bond prices will fall and the purchasing power of bond-generated income could also fall.

Interest Rate and Price Risk

Interest and price risk is very important if you want to sell a bond before its maturity. If you bought a bond at $1,000 par with a yield of 5% and the price falls, the market interest rate will rise but your bond would be worth less than when you bought it. Thus, if you sold it under these circumstances you may lose some of your principal. If you have held the bond for a long enough period of time where it has paid interest, you may be able to sell it at a lower price and break even or lose some money. The flip side is that if the price of the bond rises, you may be able to sell it at a higher price. To make sense of this, just calculate how much interest you would gain by the time the bond matures and add this figure to the current market price of the bond. If your goal is to hold the bond until maturity, your price and rate risk is usually minimal, unless the bond defaults.

Managing Income Risk

In order to diminish the potential losses from inflation or from having to sell a bond before maturity, or to have a bond called, there are two things that you can do. One is to have the right mix of bonds in the portfolio. A good recommendation for an ultra-safe, low-maintenance bond portfolio is to exclusively use U.S. Treasury bonds, or mutual funds that invest in U.S. Treasury bonds in a mixture that is composed of 50% intermediate-term bonds, 30% short-term bonds, and the remaining 20% in inflation-protected bonds called TIPS.

The second, more labor-intensive approach is a technique called laddering. That's where you buy bonds of different maturities and stagger them so that your income stream remains stable. As one bond matures, you roll over the proceeds into the next bond. The key step in laddering a portfolio is to know the current inflation rate and to structure the portfolio so that the overall interest rate that it provides is above the inflation rate. An excellent tutorial on bond laddering can be found at Fidelity Investments at: *www.fidelity.com/fixed-income-bonds/fixed-income-tools-services/bond-ladder-tool.*

Corporate Credit Check: Know the Bond Ratings

The financial analysts at Standard & Poor's, Moody's, and other agencies review, research, and rate corporate and municipal bonds. The ratings are indicative of credit worthiness or the ability of the issuer to pay. Think of the ratings as a report card of the issuer, similar to an individual's credit rating. When rating bonds, analysts look at the past payment record, the financial situation of the company, and the degree of risk associated with the bond. Issuers with the highest bond ratings are the most likely to make good on their debt. At the same time, the highest-rated bonds are the ones that are likely to pay the lowest interest rates.

The Bond Ratings Alphabet

The highest-rated bonds are rated AAA. The market considers AAA, AA, A, or BBB bonds rated by S&P as good quality. Moody's issues Aaa, Aa, A, and Bbb ratings. Bonds rated BB or Bb are considered lower quality and higher risk. Bonds with ratings below B are known as junk bonds. These pay significantly higher interest rates, but have a higher risk of default. Sometimes taking the risks offered by junk bonds pays off. But, in this sector of the bond universe, default is not unheard of.

ALERT

The best-known bond default–related crash was the stock market crash of 1987. The now-defunct financial firm Drexel Burnham Lambert underwrote and aggressively marketed junk bonds that paid such high interest rates that they were nearly irresistible. They sold these to institutions known as "savings and loans," which used the yields to attract savers to high yielding CDs. The problem was that the companies who issued the bonds could never make those interest payments for the life of the loans. As a result, the junk bond market collapsed, and the damage spread to the stock market and the banking system, especially the savings and loans sector.

Ratings Variability and the Tough Decisions

Bond ratings can change over time depending on the fortunes of the issuer. If a company offers BBB rated bonds but its operations improve, their bond ratings may change to A or higher. This may increase the appeal of their bonds. If a company starts having problems, their bond rating may fall below BBB (Bbb). That's when you may have to make a decision to sell. Much depends on what your plans are for the income produced by the bond and your risk tolerance. The key is not to wait too long. If the company goes into bankruptcy, you could lose all your money.

Prices and Yields

Bond prices and yields fluctuate based on market circumstances and supply and demand pressures. If you want to sell a bond, you can find yesterday's price in the bond tables of the *Wall Street Journal*, *Barron's*, or *USA Today*. In today's real-time markets, those prices are strictly historical. Yet, they do give you an idea as to what your bond might be worth and can get you started as you look for a fair price. Price tables will differ with each paper. And no one table can list every single bond, given the fact that there are millions of bonds available in the market at any one time. Your online broker will have access to bond listings, too. Full-service brokers will do a lot of the price research for you as well.

Here is the basic information that you will need and that you will find in most bond listings:

- **Coupon:** 3.125%. This is the yield that the bond carried when issued.
- **Maturity date:** 4/30/17. This is the date on which the bond matures.
- **Bid:** 106.875. This means that a buyer is offering to buy the bond for a price of $1,068.75 on a $1,000 bond. This bond has already delivered a profit of $68.75 (6.875%) to the bondholder on a par value of $1,000.
- **Ask:** 106.93. This means that a seller is willing to sell the bond for $1,069.30.

ALERT

While equities can be volatile, so can bonds. Because all financial markets are connected through the actions of the global economies and the coordinated action of central banks, the bond market can be just as volatile for active traders as is the stock market. To avoid volatility, investors should consider only buying bonds that they plan to hold until maturity. That means gravitating toward the highest-quality government bonds.

Buying and Selling Bonds

If you think that buying and selling bonds is a little difficult for a beginning investor, you're right. But it's not impossible. You can take your time, research the market, and get started when you feel comfortable. You may have to consider going through a full-service bond broker or spend a good amount of time becoming familiar with your online discount broker's bond quote and trading platform.

You can also buy U.S. Treasury bonds directly from the government by visiting TreasuryDirect (*www.treasurydirect.gov*). You can buy treasury bonds as well as U.S. Savings bonds on this website once you open your account. You can buy savings bonds through your bank as well. The great thing about savings bonds is that you can buy them for as low a price as $25 and pay no state or income taxes on the interest. Savings bonds can be bought without paying commission.

CHAPTER 8

Types of Bonds

The key to being a successful bond investor, as it is with stocks, is the understanding of how to allocate different bonds within a portfolio in order to extract the maximum return. That's what this chapter is about: providing details about the different kinds of bonds, their risk and reward potential, and how they can fit into a well-diversified portfolio of stocks, bonds, and other investments.

Categories of Bonds

Bonds are versatile assets and can be used for income, capital gains, and as a hedge to risk from other broad portfolio components such as stocks or commodities. The spectrum of offerings in the bond market is vast, ranging from government-issued bonds to corporate, municipal, and foreign instruments. Each category has its own risk reward profile, as well as peculiar tax implications. That's why it's important to know the particular ins and outs of each specific category.

Investors use bonds with two goals in mind: steady income from periodic interest payments or to protect and build up their capital stores. Generally, bonds are more predictable than stocks. You know when you will receive your interest payments and when your principal will be returned. Thus, for investors primarily looking for income, the best approach may be to own bonds that pay interest semiannually and that have a fixed interest rate until maturity.

For investors that have a known need for capital in the future, zero-coupon bonds may be the best option. With these bonds, the investor buys the bond at a deep discount below the par value of the bond. As a result he receives both the interest that has been compounded over the life of the bond and the purchase price at maturity in a lump sum.

In other words, as with all investments, before you start a bond portfolio, it makes sense to have a good understanding of what your financial needs will be, a sense of your time frame, and a plan.

U.S. Treasury Securities

The U.S. Treasury bond market is the biggest securities market in the world, with an average daily turnover of $250 billion per day. That makes it a very liquid market, and one in which you can raise cash rapidly if you need to. U.S. Treasuries are considered the safest securities in the world and are thought of by many investors as cash equivalents. That means that if you are a risk adverse investor, especially one who does not like the volatility of the stock market, and you don't mind holding on to a security for long periods of time, U.S. Treasuries may be your investment of choice. Perhaps the best attribute of U.S. Treasuries is that once you buy them, the interest rate that you will receive from that bond, until maturity, is locked in. That means that your return on investment is highly predictable. There are three kinds of treasuries:

- **Treasury bills (T-bills)** are short-term securities. Their maturities range from four weeks to one year. You can buy T-bills in $100 increments. T-bills are sold at a discount from face value. The discount is based on the interest rate paid by the bill. T-bills are sold in minimum lots of $100.
- **Treasury notes (T-notes)** are intermediate-term securities with maturities at two, five, and ten years. As with T-bills, you can buy T-notes in $100 increments. The Ten-Year U.S. Treasury Note yield (TNX) is considered the benchmark for most mortgages and longer-term loans. It is also the most widely quoted bond yield in the financial press.
- **Treasury bonds (T-bonds)** are long-term securities issued by the U.S. government. The most commonly traded T-bond is the thirty-year bond. The U.S. Treasury also offers a twenty-year bond. Long-term treasuries can be purchased at $100 increments and, like T-notes, pay interest every six months until maturity.

ALERT

While it is true that U.S. Treasury securities are considered to be "safe" investments, this notion of "safety" is most applicable to bonds that are held until maturity. Treasury bonds tend to trade, often in wide price ranges, in response to economic reports and geopolitical events. Thus, when you buy U.S. Treasuries, plan accordingly.

Municipal Bonds

These are bonds sold by cities, states, counties, and even school districts. They are also known as "munis" and are very popular investments because of their tax-free advantages. Municipalities sell munis in order to finance projects, such as building or repairing roads, bridges, schools, parks, and sports arenas. Munis are very popular because they are usually exempt from federal, and often state, taxes.

Municipal bonds are often rated by rating analysts from Standard & Poor's and Moody's via similar ratings to those used for corporate bonds. Ratings range from AAA (S&P) or Aaa (Moody's) for the highest grades to BBB or Bbb and below. When considering municipal bonds, look to own BBB rated bonds or above. As in the case of corporate bonds, the lower the rating for a municipal bond, the higher the yield, and the risk of default. With municipal bonds you can buy bond insurance in order to protect against losses.

The minimal investment for municipal bonds is $5,000, and they are then offered in multiples of $5,000. The general trends for interest rates, risk ratings, and other external factors, such as the local economy for the municipality selling the bond, affect the interest rate that any muni-bond pays investors. Prices are listed in bond tables, which are similar to those for treasury bonds. You may sell your municipal bond at a higher price than what you paid for it, but you will have to pay capital gains taxes.

If these bonds make sense for your portfolio, get to know the different types:

- **Revenue bonds.** These are bonds issued to finance specific products such as bridges, toll roads, or airports. Interest paid to investors comes from the revenues generated by the project.
- **Moral obligation bonds.** These are special circumstance revenue bonds issued by a state when it can't actually meet the bond obligation through its normal revenue stream, essentially taxes and licensing fees. In these cases, the state forms a special obligation fund that can be used to pay the bond obligation. The kicker is that the state has no legal obligation to pay bondholders from that special obligation fund; just a moral obligation. What makes this bond worth considering is that the state is actually putting its good reputation on the line, so the moral obligation is often considered more powerful in the markets than the legal obligation.
- **General obligation bonds.** These are bonds that are backed by taxes. They are also known as GOs and require voter approval. The principal is backed by the full faith and credit of the issuer.
- **Taxable municipal bonds.** If paying taxes on a municipal bond sounds crazy, consider that these bonds, despite the taxes, can offer higher

yields than comparable corporate bonds, and are generally considered to have lower risks associated with them. Common uses for this kind of muni include financing of underfunded pension plans or to build a local sports arena.

- **Private activity bonds** are used for financing both public and private activities.
- **Put bonds** allow the investor to redeem them at par value on a specific date (or dates) prior to the stated maturity. In exchange, put bonds offer lower yields than comparable municipals because of this built-in flexibility. This early out feature allows you to cash in your bond and exchange it for a higher yielding bond if you have the opportunity to do so.
- **Floating and variable rate municipal bonds** are good to own if you expect that interest will rise at some point in the future, as the bond will adjust. Because of this feature, the price of these bonds may be more volatile.

Municipal bond prices can fluctuate fairly frequently; thus, it may make sense to develop a good relationship with a muni broker and to check prices with her on a routine basis, as well as in your local newspaper, and online if you use a discount broker.

ALERT

When looking to buy municipal bonds, be thorough in your research. After the 2008 financial crisis, many municipalities encountered deep problems. Consider the problems in Hershey, Pennsylvania, and Detroit. Understand the issues that led to the problems in these two cities and use them as a model for what you don't want in a muni bond issuer.

Corporate Bonds

A corporate bond, also known as a "corporate," like all bonds, is essentially a loan agreement between a corporation and investors. And while stockholders own shares of stocks, which are pieces of a company, by contrast, corporate bondholders are moneylenders to the company that issues the bond. Bondholders lend money to companies for a specific amount of time and a specified rate of interest. Corporate bonds tend to be riskier investments than treasury or municipal bonds but, when properly chosen, have historically outperformed other bonds.

Corporates pay a higher interest rate because the issuing companies generally have a higher risk of default than governments and municipalities, although after the Great Recession, that is not as hard and fast a rule since Greece and several U.S. cities went bankrupt after the 2007–2008 financial crisis. Recent corporate bankruptcies include the European car company Saab, U.S. auto giant Chrysler, and American Airlines. Corporate bondholders in those companies all took losses when the companies defaulted on their bonds during bankruptcy proceedings.

ALERT

Corporate bonds are not insured. If you are a safety prone investor, this type of investment may not make sense for you. Another alternative may be to consider a mutual fund that invests in corporate bonds. By owning shares in the fund you will diversify, but not totally avoid risk of default.

Corporate Bond Checklist

Here are some key points to consider with corporate bonds:

- Corporate bonds are issued in multiples of either $1,000 or $5,000. They are rated by S&P and Moody's using the AAA- or Aaa-based system described earlier in this chapter.
- Income and capital gains associated with corporate bonds are fully taxable at federal and state levels.
- Interest is paid annually or semiannually.
- If your goal is to invest in highly rated, high-quality corporate bonds from blue chip companies, and you hold the bond until maturity, there is a reasonable, but not guaranteed, chance that you will not face risk of losing your money due to a bond payment default.

Bond Calls

When a bond is called, it means that the issuer is redeeming the bond before maturity. The most common reason is that by calling in the bond and reissuing it at a lower interest rate, the issuing entity will save money. Only bonds that have a call provision can be called early. The call provision describes the details and conditions that allow the early redemption. For example, a fifteen-year bond may be called as early as eight years into its lifespan. If you reinvest in a called bond, usually issued at a lower interest rate, your return will be different than that of the original bond.

Sinking-Fund Provision

A sinking-fund provision is when a company retires a certain number of bonds per year by using its earnings, when the funds become available for such a purpose. Bonds with sinking-fund provision features must state that this is a part of the deal. The company, depending on its current circumstances, chooses bonds to be retired via this maneuver. Thus, your bond may or may not get chosen. If your bond gets chosen, you may lose money.

The bottom line is that corporate bonds have their positive and negative sides. Higher yields also mean higher risk. The possibility of a company bankruptcy, or of a quirky callable feature of the bond, makes it mandatory that you read everything very carefully before investing.

Zero-Coupon Bonds

Companies, governments, and government agencies, as well as municipalities, can issue zero-coupon bonds. Zeros do not make periodic interest rate payments. Instead, you buy them at a deep discount and receive a higher rate lump sum (both interest and principal) when the bond reaches maturity. The only reason to own zeros is because they allow you to plan for that lump sum at maturity. Thus, they are ideal for retirement planning. The downside is that even though you don't receive interest payments, you must report the amount of appreciation of the bond every year for tax purposes.

Here is how they work. If you bought a ten-year $10,000 zero municipal bond, you may pay $5,000. In ten years you would receive $10,000. The longer the time to maturity, the deeper the purchase price is discounted and the greater the return based on compounding of the interest that is not being paid.

High-Yield Bonds

High-yield bonds, also known as junk bonds, can provide a higher return, but often offer a higher risk of default or of a rapid fall in price. That's because the companies that issue these bonds have lower credit ratings than other companies; thus, their bonds get lower ratings from the ratings agencies. In order to attract investors, they have to pay a higher interest rate.

FACT

Wall Street likes to use "comfort" words. By calling a junk bond a high-yield bond, the issuers are hoping that you are not going to be frightened away. Don't be fooled. Junk is junk, and you should be wary of these bonds unless you are a well-diversified, well-financed, experienced investor.

Often the reason for the low credit rating is that the company is at some stage of restructuring or because the company is merging with another and the bonds are part of the financing for the merger. In some cases, the bondholder may suffer from factors that affect the price of the company's stock. In these situations, not only may the bond lose value quickly, but it may also lose its liquidity and be very difficult to sell.

At other times, a company that issues junk bonds in its early growth stages improves its operations and is able to improve its credit rating, thus issuing higher-grade bonds in the future. This would be a situation where the company calls the lower-grade bonds in order to issue higher-grade bonds that pay lower interest rates. What that means for you is that you may get the high rate for a shorter period than you may expect.

This is a special situation that you may want to watch for. Buy the high-yield bonds of a young company that shows signs of growing into a company with staying power. You may enjoy the higher rates for a period of time and then, when the high-yield bond is called, you may consider whether you want to buy the higher-grade bond that is issued in its place. No matter what you do, understand that high-yield bonds are known as junk bonds for a reason, and that reason is that a fair amount of the time, they are just that: junk.

Mortgage-Backed Securities

Mortgage-backed securities (MBS) are bonds backed by mortgage payments. And until 2007, they were considered among the safest areas of the bond market. That's because it was widely believed that Americans would always pay their mortgage and that home prices would continue to rise. But this former "safe" haven in the bond market turned into a disaster area in 2007 and 2008 as the "subprime" mortgage became synonymous with the near collapse of the global economy. In fact, the take-home message for beginning investors should be to avoid this sector altogether.

The major reason, aside from its high risk, is that it's a complex sector that often involves interest rates that are collected in derivative instruments known as collateralized mortgage obligations (CMOs), where more than one mortgage is pooled together in order to collect the capital to make the interest rate.

Consider that when you buy a corporate, municipal, or treasury bond, you only have to deal with one issuer. In these cases, you only have to look to one payer—the U.S. Treasury, a city, or a corporation—to make good on its promise to pay. Now, compare this to the path of a typical MBS. A bank sells the mortgage to the homeowner. Then the bank sells the mortgage to a servicing firm. Then, in order for investors to receive their interest payments, the homeowner must make his mortgage payment to the servicing firm, who holds the mortgage. The servicing firm collects the money from individuals, then allocates the money to each particular pool or CMO, and then from that pool, it pays the interest to investors. That is clearly a situation in which there are too many steps in the chain of custody of the money. And the more steps, the more there is a chance for something to go wrong. Which is what happened in 2007 and why the whole industry collapsed when the crucial step in the chain, the mortgage holder, stopped making payments.

FACT

As the real estate boom of the early 2000s slowed, in order to continue their earning streams, mortgage lenders began to sell mortgages to very high-risk clients. These included sales to people whose income and future prospects, under normal circumstances, would not qualify them for certain loans. As a result, and as common sense would suggest, those buyers stopped making payments and the boom became a bust. Here is an interesting statistic: Subprime mortgages, those linked to the 2007–2008 mortgage collapse, only made up 25 percent of all mortgages issued prior to the crash.

If you have an interest in these kinds of bonds, consider investing in a mutual fund that holds the highest-rated MBS loans, those guaranteed by the Government National Mortgage Association (GNMA). Otherwise, look elsewhere.

The Bond Investor Checklist

Diversification is the key to success in bond investing. By owning multiple types of bonds of differing characteristics and laddering your portfolio, through holding a range of different maturities, you can limit the volatility of your bond holdings. Your bond ladder should have an average maturity that coincides with your financial goals and your time range. Bonds are not without risk. Before buying bonds, also consider the following:

- Tax implications. Consider whether tax-free municipal bonds make sense in your portfolio. Review, with your CPA, the potential risks of hidden taxes, including that of triggering the AMT (alternative minimum tax) rules. And look into the potential consequences of owning zero-coupon bonds before you invest in them.
- Consider the inflation effect of your bond holdings. If your overall portfolio is well insulated from inflation, you may be able to avoid taking extra risks with your bond portfolio.
- Safety first. A high-quality portfolio may not give the best return in dollar terms. But the peace of mind and the stability of such a set of holdings,

in most cases, are well worth the potential loss of gain that comes with taking too much risk.

- Remember that your bond portfolio has multiple purposes. Aside from providing income, the other important function of a well-structured bond portfolio is to provide stability to the overall investment portfolio when stocks become volatile.
- Junk is junk and mortgages sometimes go unpaid. Don't chase high-yield bonds just to make more money in the short term. Avoid most junk bonds, and if you must own mortgage-backed securities, consider a GNMA mutual fund.

CHAPTER 9

The Mutual Fund: The Beginner's Best Friend

If there were ever a financial instrument ideally suited to a beginning investor, it would be the mutual fund. Created in Europe in the mid-1800s, mutual funds hit the American shores when Harvard University created the first American pooled fund. Initially ridiculed, mutual funds now house billions of dollars of money and are major contributors to market activity as well as shareholder financial reward. This chapter is all about mutual funds and how they can be a significant part of your portfolio.

What Is a Mutual Fund?

A mutual fund is a registered investment company that sells shares to investors and invests the pooled assets of all shareholders in the markets on their behalf. A mutual fund share's price is the net asset value (NAV) and is the result of the mutual fund's total assets divided by the number of outstanding shares. Thus, a mutual fund with $10 million in total assets and one million shares outstanding has a NAV of $10.

Mutual funds are excellent investment vehicles for beginning investors. They let you partcipate in the market, but also provide a certain comfort level. Many investors that start their endeavors by using mutual funds move on to stocks, options, and futures. You may be one of them. The key is to take your time and transition to higher risk, higher work requirement investments when you're ready.

FACT

Mutual funds are managed by professionals, whose job it is to invest the fund's assets on behalf of their shareholders.

Some Fund Facts

If you are considering becoming a mutual fund investor, you are not alone and you'll have a whole lot of choices. According to the most recent data from the Investment Company Institute (*www.icifactbook.org/fb_data.html*), as of April 2014, there were 9,608 mutual funds that invested directly in some kind of financial market in the United States. The list did not include mutual funds that invest in other mutual funds, which are also known as funds of funds. Forty-seven percent (47%) of those mutual funds invested in stocks, while 20% invested in bonds, including treasuries, corporates, high-yield, and municipal bonds. There were 580 (6%) money market mutual funds in the list and 540 (roughly another 6%) funds that invested in stocks, bonds, and other assets combined.

But things have changed some in the industry. Consider that in 2006, the total number of mutual funds was over 10,000 and that in 1991, there were only 3,000 mutual funds in existence. So, while the number of mutual funds may have topped out, it has still tripled in the last decade and a half. As a result we can infer both that Americans are investing through mutual funds, and that the numbers may be shifting (a sign that investors became gun-shy after the 2008 bear market).

Growth of Hybrid Funds

While the number of equity mutual funds and the total number of bond funds decreased after 2008, the number of hybrid funds, those that invest in a mix of assets, grew. That suggests that the investors who stayed in the markets are likely to have changed their strategies away from owning equity and bond mutual funds separately and have now shifted assets to mutual funds that do the asset allocation for them. In other words, Americans are leaving the big investment and asset allocation decisions to someone else. And the strategy seems to have worked for them. Although the overall number of mutual fund accounts topped out in 2007, the assets held in mutual funds grew to over $13 billion by the end of 2012.

Why Mutual Fund Investing Is a Good Thing for Investors

Mutual funds add a layer of protection between the market and the investors. It is not a foolproof safety net, but it does come in handy. This protection is composed of two things: diversification and convenience.

Diversification

Because the fund manager picks stocks and adjusts their contribution to the fund's return, you don't have to. That means that your risk is spread beyond a handful of stocks. If a mutual fund can diversify into bonds and other asset classes, this can also add another layer of diversification and protect you from excessive volatility in stocks. Add to this the fact that because the mutual fund has large sums of money, it can buy larger lots of stocks, often with discounted commissions, a fact that can cut your costs. The net effect is that mutual funds can cut your costs, balance your risk, and let you participate in bull markets.

You can add another layer of diversification to your mutual fund portfolio by owning more than one category. For example, you can balance the potential risk that can come with an aggressive growth stock fund by also owning shares in a conservative treasury bond fund. You can also monitor hot sectors in the market and trade in and out of sector-specific funds that are acting well. If international funds are acting well, you may want to own some shares there as well. A fund that specializes in real estate and a precious metals and commodity fund may also be worth considering. But be careful. You can also overdo your fund diversification. Owning more than five to seven mutual funds at any one time is likely to increase your risk as well as possibly duplicating some of your holdings. Your goal when diversifying your fund holdings is to balance risk for your portfolio. No matter how good your fund manager may be, if he is a stock picker, he will always pick stocks. That means that when stocks fall, the price of most stock funds will fall with the market. This holds true for bond funds when bonds retreat and for all funds in any class.

In fact, before investing, be aware that mutual funds are not guaranteed to make money. And, unless the fund manager is truly nimble and can move all of the funds' holdings to a safe asset allocation in times of trouble, you will lose some money in any type of mutual fund during bad markets in any asset class. Yet over time, owning a portfolio of well-diversified, well-managed mutual funds can be a pretty good deal for most investors. Above all, mutual funds are convenient, given the fact that as an investor, you need to pick and monitor the fund as it pertains to your needs, goals, and financial plan. Thankfully, you don't have to manage the entire fund's portfolio.

Is It All about the Fund Manager?

Mutual fund companies, like any other business, try to find ways to attract customers. A successful mutual fund may be marketed by associating it with a charismatic manager. Peter Lynch, the ex-manager of Fidelity's Magellan Fund (FMAGX) became a legend in the 1980s and is considered by many to be the best mutual fund manager of all time. Under his guidance, Magellan averaged 29% yearly returns for thirteen years. Magellan delivered such heady gains for its shareholders during that period that Lynch became a media star, writing books, making talk show appearances, and retiring a wealthy man. Lynch is responsible for the investment approach described earlier in this book, "Buy What You Know and Know What You Buy" in Chapter 5. He remains a consultant to Fidelity Investments, but Magellan is now a decent, not an exceptional, mutual fund. Most notably, the fund lost nearly 50% of its value during the year 2008, although it rebounded well in 2009 when the market finally bottomed.

The point of telling this story is that a fund manager, no matter how good he is, is at the mercy of the markets. Lynch was an excellent manager. But he also had the best of times in which to ply his wares. As an investor, you have to weigh the performance of the manager, but you must also temper your expectations based on market conditions.

ALERT

Fund managers can be sketchy. Beware of clever marketing by mutual funds, especially when the focus of the advertising is the fund manager. If the manager is a celebrity, make sure that his results also measure up.

Evaluating Your Fund Manager

When reviewing a fund manager's performance:

- Look at several years of returns. If the fund has been delivering consistent returns during the manager's tenure, look at other funds that she has managed. If the performance comparison yields consistent returns, especially through good and bad markets, you've found a good manager.
- Compare the fund's performance to the market during both up and down years. See what the fund did when the stock market crashed in 2008 and how fast it rebounded and to what degree. This will tell you a lot about what you may expect in the future, as there will be other bad markets to manage through.
- Make sure that the manager is adhering to his fund's investment strategy. If you are looking for a conservative strategy and your review of the fund's latest report shows that there are mostly momentum stocks in the

portfolio, you need to consider whether the fund is what you are looking for.

- Look into whether the manager is a lone wolf or has a management team. If she is a lone wolf, the fund may suffer when she moves on and does not leave anyone at the helm that could emulate the successful strategy and deliver the kinds of returns that you may expect. If the performance of the fund is similar regardless of the manager, and it suits your goals, you've found a match.

Mutual Fund Families

There are many mutual fund families of different sizes. But in an industry of thousands, there are several giant firms that between them gobble up most of the market share: Fidelity, Vanguard, Pimco, American, Franklin Templeton, Invesco, and BlackRock are usually near the top when you rank mutual fund companies by assets under management. These are not the only mutual fund companies, but these big companies offer a wide variety of funds in the growth, growth and income, hybrid, and asset allocation categories, and that makes them a good place to start your search. They also offer plenty of options in the bond categories, ranging from treasuries to high-yield. Some are specialists. For example, Pimco is primarily a bond mutual fund company, while the others offer a large variety of fund choices. Franklin Templeton specializes in international markets, while Fidelity has a very large selection of mutual funds with a specialization in industry sector-specific mutual funds.

There are also niche players that cater to a particular clientele, such as the Rydex and ProFunds families. These two families specialize in offering mutual funds to investors who like to switch between mutual funds on a regular basis, often on a daily basis. These two fund families also offer mutual funds that sell the markets short, or rise when the underlying assets fall in price.

When choosing a mutual fund family, consider the following:

- **Reputation:** Research whether the company has had any significant legal or enforcement actions against it in the past five years and whether there are any pending legal actions against it. If a mutual fund company turns up in the news as being investigated due to accounting problems and undergoes frequent management changes, these are red flags that should tell you to go somewhere else.

- **Primary business:** If a mutual fund company is part of a large financial conglomerate such as a bank, mutual funds may or may not be their primary focus. That may make a big difference in fees, performance, and customer service.
- **Performance:** Look at mutual fund ratings in each family during good and bad markets and review how the company's funds have fared. Consistently good results are preferable to outstanding years once in a blue moon.
- **Investment approach:** Review the overall philosophy of the fund family and how it matches your own personality and risk profile. If you are a patient conservative investor, you may find a good fit in Vanguard, a company that frowns on investors who like to switch in and out of mutual funds frequently. If you are someone who might enjoy the mutual fund switching investment approach, you may do well with Rydex or ProFunds.

FACT

There are two great sources of information on mutual funds. First is the Investment Company Institute (*www.ici.org*). The second is Lipper (*www.lipperweb.com*). The Investment Company Institute is the mutual fund industry group that chronicles the industry and keeps all the statistics and facts about mutual funds. Lipper is a great resource for those looking for more current information about mutual funds, especially with regard to performance.

Expenses, Loads, and Other Fees

Mutual funds have expenses. Aside from trading commissions, mutual funds pay rent for office space and may have other operational real estate and expenses. As with any company, mutual funds also have employees who require salaries and benefits. Fund managers often travel to personally "kick the tires" of a company that they are evaluating for investment purposes.

And since shareholders are the major source of income for the company, they will pay for the cost of all the things that are required to run the fund.

Load or No Load?

The first fee to consider is the "load," or the fee that an advisor receives from the fund company for selling you a mutual fund. A "no load" mutual fund that you find yourself has at least an equal chance of being as good as a load fund. Some special cases of load funds sold directly to investors are sector funds. Because these funds may have higher expenses, since they cater to investors who may not hold them for extended periods of time, mutual fund companies may charge a load for them. As a general rule, though, there is no hard and fast rule that says that load funds are better than no-load funds. Be careful when you buy no-load funds, though. They may have hidden fees in them that could surprise you if you didn't expect them.

Digging Into Fee Details

Before investing, look at the expense ratio part of the prospectus. Some companies are trickier than others, but most of the large families are fairly straightforward in their language. If there is something that you don't understand in the fee structure, it makes sense to stop and look it up. You don't want to get charged any more than necessary by a mutual fund company.

Here are some typical fees:

- **Service fees:** These are fees used to pay the salaries, commissions, and consulting fees of financial planners, analysts, and brokers who service the customers and provide support services to clients on behalf of the fund company.
- **Administrative fees:** These are the fees from which the mutual fund company pays for office space, staff salaries, and office equipment and funds the general cost of running the business. These fees also include the cost of online support, check processing, auditing, record keeping, and the production and printing of brochures and shareholder reports. In some cases, the funds absorb these fees into their management fees.

- **Management fees:** This is the fee that goes to the fund manager, expressed as a percentage. Some funds have flat percentage fees, while others vary the fee based on the fund's return. As a general rule, the larger the fund, the lower the management fee percentage.
- **12b-1 fee:** This fee, which is usually between 0.25% and 1% on an annual basis, is used to pay for the fund's advertising. This fee can be seen as unnecessary, or you can agree with the funds, whose point of view is that by advertising they get more clients and the overall costs of running the fund go down over time.

Total expense ratios for a mutual fund can range from 0.25% to as high as 2.5%. You have to pay attention to this as it can sap your returns. If your fund has a high expense ratio and a poor return, find a new one.

ESSENTIAL

You can buy no-load, low-load fees directly. The remarkable thing is that high-load mutual funds with big expenses don't often perform any better than their no-load brethren. Make sure you can justify paying big bucks for flashy funds.

Making Sense of Fund Reports

Your mutual fund's annual or semiannual reports are important tools to help you measure performance. Pay special attention to the section that details the fund's holdings in order to keep tabs on the fund's manager. A manager whose style "drifts" from the fund's stated objectives could be a sign of trouble. If your fund's objective is small-cap growth, and you see large holdings of Apple, Google, and Coca-Cola, your manager is showing signs of "style drifting."

Before deciding whether this is a positive or a negative, though, consider why the manager may be changing the objective. Is it because the market is changing? Or is it because he is chasing performance and the large-cap stocks are acting better in the current market than the small-cap growth stocks that he is supposed to be investing in? Check how other small-cap growth funds are doing and compare. If your fund is doing better, it may make sense to keep it, as long as you keep an eye on it, in comparison to other funds that invest in the same general area of the market.

Here are some things to look for in these reports:

- **Familiar names:** Look for companies that fit the bill of the fund. If there aren't many that you recognize, dig deeper. Try to get in your manager's head. If your research shows that your fund manager is heavily invested in South African mining companies, this may be a much higher risk mutual fund than you want.

- **Portfolio concentration:** If your fund is overweight in a particular sector, you should look into that sector and see if its fundamentals warrant that kind of exposure. If your manager is loading up on biotech or bank stocks, research the sectors carefully. Your fund manager may be onto something. Or he may be heading for trouble. At the end of the day, it's all about whether you're getting what the fund advertises and how comfortable you are with what the manager is doing.

- **Compare your fund to the right benchmark:** The report should list the fund's performance in comparison to the appropriate benchmark. If the report of your small-cap growth fund is comparing its performance solely to the Ten-Year U.S. Treasury Note, you may have a problem. To be sure, funds often compare their performance to that of their traditional benchmark index or sector, as well as that of treasuries. The point is that small-cap fund performance should be compared to a small-cap benchmark such as the Russell 2000 Index.

The report should also explain why the fund manager made the decisions reflected in his holdings, why they worked out or didn't fare well, and what he plans to do about it in the future. If you're scratching your head after reading the report, especially after a period of underperformance, you may need to get another fund.

Finally, know that the annual report is important, but you don't have to wait for it to make a decision about your fund or to know its performance. You can check your fund's performance as often as you like in your morning paper, online, or by calling the mutual fund company's toll-free number. Fund companies usually post the fund's closing price, usually after 5:00 P.M.

EST, in a recorded message. Some companies have password access lines where you can punch in mutual fund codes to get the price.

Different Approaches to Mutual Fund Investing

Now that you're ready to invest, it's time to consider your mutual fund share buying and style choices. As with any other form of investing, how you go about buying and selling is dictated by your personality, your risk profile, and your time frame. At the end of the day, though, the most important factor is how you can make money by investing in mutual funds.

FACT

To open a mutual fund account directly with a company, you can visit a local investor center or get an account application by phone. You then fill it out and include your check, and usually within a few days to a couple of weeks, your account is set up and you can start buying and selling shares.

At its core, mutual fund investing is similar to stock investing. You buy shares in a mutual fund in hopes of selling them at a higher price or net asset value at some point in the future. If you buy shares in a fund, and it doesn't appreciate in price over a reasonable period of time, based on your time frame, personality, and needs, you simply sell the shares. Before you buy shares, make sure that you know of any limits or fees that may apply when you buy or sell shares. When selling mutual fund shares, you must consider the effect of fees for redeeming shares in less than the allotted time. These fees are called exit loads. Mutual funds charge these fees in order to minimize the effect of large numbers of redemptions on the fund's capital. Your fund will inform you, in its prospectus, if there are any such fees and how they apply. No-load funds have no upfront or back-end loads. Most mutual funds, load and no load, limit the number of times that you can sell shares per year. This number varies per fund and per fund family.

Dollar Cost Averaging: Buying During Good and Bad Times

Dollar cost averaging is an investment method that is well suited for long-term mutual fund investing. You do this by investing a fixed sum of money into a mutual fund periodically. Some investors opt to buy a fixed number of shares. The fixed sum of money method tends to work better, due to price fluctuations in fund shares. Many investors dollar cost average every month or every quarter. The net effect is that, over time, you build a large number of shares in the fund. Sometimes you buy shares for lower prices and sometimes at higher prices, depending on the overall market. This method works well for IRAs, 401(k) plans, and other retirement plans.

Dollar cost averaging often makes the most sense in the beginning of your investment plan. This helps you get into the habit of saving as well as offering the potential for building up your assets. It's more about discipline than the amount you put in. One good way to compromise is to have a minimum contribution and a set schedule. If you decide that you will buy $200 worth of shares in a mutual fund every month, then stick to it. If you have more on some months, it may be worth your while to put in a bit more when you have it. The key is to stick to the routine and to build assets.

Dollar cost averaging is the opposite of market timing, the style of investing that attempts to buy at specific times during market periods. For example, market timers look to buy when markets have been falling for some time and their market timing indicators are flashing signals that this may be a good moment to buy. Market timers also look to sell before a market falls. The goal of market timers is to make the most money possible when markets are trending and to sell before the trend changes. There are whole books devoted to market timing. It can be done, but it is difficult and can be a risky proposition.

Dollar cost averaging can also be emotionally difficult, as it requires putting money into fund shares even during bear markets. If you can stomach this aspect of the technique, and you have enough time for things to work out, this is a good approach to mutual fund investing.

CHAPTER 10

The Large Universe of Mutual Funds

In a universe where you have 10,000 choices, it pays to know your stuff. The broader your understanding of the different kinds of mutual funds—stocks, bonds, hybrid, and sector specific—the better off you'll be and the better your chances of making good decisions. Each type of fund, whether it invests in stocks, bonds, or a mixture of assets, has a potential place in your fund. How you choose them and how you allocate your money within them has to do with your personality, your risk profile, and the amount of time and effort that you are willing to give your portfolio. This chapter will help you make intelligent choices in your mutual fund investing. The most important fact to know is that your return will be based on the performance of the financial class in which the fund invests, whether it's stocks, bonds, or a mixture of multiple asset classes.

Index Funds

Index funds are designed to match the performance of a specific index. To do this, the funds buy the same assets or securities in identical proportions to the index. The most common and best-known index mutual funds mimic the S&P 500. Index funds are passively managed, meaning that there is little trading and asset shifting, which means lower fees for you. Historically, the S&P 500 outperformed 81% of all equity funds. From 2001 to 2007, the S&P trailed about half of actively managed equity mutual funds. In the bear market of 2008, the S&P 500 outperformed all actively managed funds except for large-cap managed equity funds.

Index funds are attractive because they offer:

- **Ease of investing:** You know exactly what you're getting. When you buy an S&P 500 index fund, you expect to earn market style results at a low cost.
- **Variety:** There are many mutual funds that track other indexes, such as small-cap and mid-cap stocks and industry sectors. For example, if you want to own technology stocks, you can buy a mutual fund that tracks a technology index such as Vanguard Information Technology Index Fund (VITAX).
- **Diversification:** A selection of index mutual funds can help you create your own diversified fund portfolio. A good mix may be a large-cap index fund that tracks the Dow Jones Industrial Average or the S&P 500, coupled with a mid-cap mutual fund that tracks the S&P MidCap 400 Index and an index fund that tracks the Russell 2000 Index of small-cap stocks. You can add some safety by adding a treasury bond index mutual fund and a sector mutual fund that tracks a gold stock benchmark or a commodity index.

Growth Funds Versus Income Funds

There are two ways to make money: by growing capital gains and by receiving income. Growth stocks appreciate in price while income securities pay dividends, and there are mutual funds that specialize in either approach, separately or simultaneously. As you will see, there is no reason to choose between these two general categories of funds. Each type has a place in your portfolio, and an appropriate blend of both tends to make for a more stable and less volatile portfolio during tough markets.

ESSENTIAL

Beginning investors can benefit by owning both growth and income mutual funds. By combining the two categories they can have portfolio diversification and possible protection of assets when one or the other type of fund runs into difficulties due to market trend changes.

Growth Funds

Mutual funds that specialize in growth stocks are not as interested in the current price of a stock. Instead, they focus on stocks with the potential to appreciate in price. These funds will buy any stock at any price if their analysis suggests that the price will rise, even from levels that have already risen significantly. Thus, growth funds tend to gravitate toward higher risk momentum stocks that can move significantly higher for relatively long periods of time, such as months or even years.

These mutual funds are interested in stocks with extraordinary potential for gains, especially those with new products that are creating new social trends. Think of Apple, Google, and Facebook in their growth sweet spots as well as their future counterparts, and you've got the commonly held type of stocks in these mutual funds. Long-term growth funds tend to focus on more mature growth companies that still have potential, while aggressive growth funds look for the "next big deal" companies earlier in the cycle.

Capital Appreciation Funds

A name for the most aggressive of growth stock mutual funds is capital appreciation. These are the most aggressive of all mutual funds, and when they are doing well they usually hit home runs. That's because they focus solely on momentum stocks, or stocks that have exceptional growth potential in the short run. What that means is that when the momentum runs out, these funds can be at the bottom of the performance lists.

Income Funds

Income funds are all about stocks that pay dividends, which are passed to the fund's shareholders. Some of these funds may also hold bonds in order to increase their income producing potential. If you reinvest your dividends, you will build the number of shares you hold. It's a good idea to check the tax consequences of owning these funds with your CPA, as you are likely to be taxed. If you hold these funds in a retirement account, the income's tax effect will be deferred. These funds tend to be more stable in down or volatile markets. But don't let this general tendency of the category lull you into a false sense of security. In the age of high frequency trading, any stock can become volatile.

Combined Growth and Income Funds

If you have a small portfolio and are looking for a one-stop shop, a combined growth and income fund is the one for you. By combining growth stocks, dividend-paying stocks, and even a few bonds, this kind of mutual fund is often capable of delivering excellent results with the added advantage of being less volatile. Growth and income managers tend to be more cautious in the kinds of stocks that they pick, and balance the more aggressive picks with steady dividend payers and often a sprinkling of bonds in order to deliver steady returns in rising stock markets and decrease the potential for losses in down markets. This may also be a good fund for early retirees who still want to have some money in the stock market but are looking to be more conservative.

Value Funds

Value mutual funds invest in shares of companies that are undervalued. That means that the companies in these funds are usually struggling, or are at least perceived to be struggling by the market when the value fund manager is buying their shares. But while the appeal of a value stock may be low, the reason the stock is underperforming may be as simple as the fact that its product cycle has hit a dull period or that it's undergoing a change in management. Thus, a big part of value investing is the understanding of the company, its fundamentals, and the reason why the market has not recognized its future potential. Value mutual funds, however, are not necessarily market laggards. A good value manager recognizes future growth potential in an undervalued stock, then seeks to buy the stock cheap so that he can ride the stock's next up cycle when the growth managers get clued in to the story and start to buy it. So don't be fooled by the category's name. Value funds aren't likely to be wallflowers during bull markets. If the fund manager did his job right, he picked good value stocks in the past that are participating in any stock market rally in the present. As the stock rises in price and the valuation rises, the manager will sell his position and put the money to work in other underperforming stocks with the goal of repeating the feat.

ESSENTIAL

Some value funds can deliver results that are comparable to aggressive growth funds. This is usually due to both good times for this kind of investing as well as good portfolio management. Even for growth investors, it's a good idea to, at least, monitor the performance of a few value funds at any time as it may make sense to put some money in a value fund that has a hot hand.

Considering Sector Funds

Sector funds are ideal for investors who like to trade based on technical analysis and momentum, and have variable time frames ranging from days to weeks, or weeks to months. These mutual funds buy stocks in a single sector of the market, such as health care, technology, or energy. There are even specialized funds that focus on information technology, natural gas stocks, and not just all banks, but regional banks. Generally, the narrower the focus of a sector, the greater its tendency to be volatile and the higher the risk potential that it offers. Still, if you are a risk taker and like momentum, sector funds are likely for you. A simple strategy is to put together a list of sector funds. An easy place to start is with the Fidelity Select funds. You can find them listed in the mutual fund section of *Investor's Business Daily* or the *Wall Street Journal*. Get in the habit of checking them periodically. You can chart them on StockCharts.com, see which ones are interesting, and consider whether owning shares in one or more of them makes sense.

FACT

Sector funds can deliver hefty gains. A great example was the run of Fidelity Select Health Care (FSPHX) in the eight years from January 1993 to December 2000, which delivered a nearly 300% gain to shareholders. Although this is not necessarily typical, it is not all that rare if you can find the fund that is at the center of a significant trend. This fund capitalized on what many in the health-care field call the golden age of cholesterol reducing drugs, which produced huge earnings for pharmaceutical companies and drove their shares to incredible gains.

Balanced Funds and Built-In Asset Allocation

While growth and income funds offer some asset allocation, balanced funds and asset allocation funds go all the way, putting together a portfolio of stocks, bonds, and cash under one roof. Balanced funds tend to gravitate toward stocks and bonds, while asset allocation funds split the portfolio into stocks, bonds, and short-term instruments like treasury bills and short-term bonds. These are ideal for investors who want to buy a mutual fund and worry about it as little as possible because, in this case, the manager literally does all of the worrying. This doesn't mean that you should abandon the fund to its own devices. You should read the annual report and see what the manager is doing. And you should pay attention to the fund's performance during all markets.

Here are three things to expect from a balanced or asset allocation fund:

- **Performance:** If the stock market is on a very hot streak, your balanced fund should be participating, perhaps not to the degree of an aggressive growth fund, but it should certainly be moving in the same general trend as the stock market.
- **Safety:** The goal of a balanced portfolio is to reduce risk. That means that if the stock market is falling hard, your balanced fund should be falling less due to its bond and cash components.

- **Consistency and predictability:** Although no mutual fund can have identical performance during any two different periods of time, more than growth funds, the balanced and asset allocator funds should be able to smooth out market volatility to a reasonable degree while delivering better returns than cash.

International and Global Funds

Globalization has created investment opportunities in established economies, such as Europe, and emerging markets, such as those of Asia and Latin America. There are, however, some important distinctions to keep in mind when investing in these funds. Global funds may include U.S. securities in the mix, while international funds will not. The name of the fund will describe the region(s) in which the fund invests. Consider these factors when investing in foreign-focused mutual funds:

- The risk tends to be higher in international funds, but the rewards can also be high, given any current economical trends. Funds that invested in South America did well in the 1990s. The twenty-first century tended to favor Chinese investments. The key when investing in this type of fund is to find the dominant trend of where money is flowing.
- The narrower the focus of the fund, the greater the chance of volatility will be. Funds that invest in a single country are more likely to have wider price fluctuations than funds that invest in a region or a continent. For example, a fund that invests in Europe may be more stable than a fund that invests only in Bulgaria.
- The global economy is essentially connected. That means that a change in the trend in the U.S. economy will also likely affect foreign markets. That means that these funds may not provide any added safety if you are looking to escape from a problem in the United States.
- If global trends continue in the same general direction over the next five to ten years, we may see more conflicts, a higher potential for wars, and a rise in the number of periods of instability in the global economy. Beginning investors should use these funds only for diversification purposes and consider only using them as a small portion of their portfolio.

Small-Cap, Mid-Cap, and Large-Cap Funds

In the stock market and the world of mutual funds, the word "cap" means "capitalization," or the market value of the company. Large-cap mutual funds invest in the better-known large companies. Mid-cap funds invest in smaller but not small companies. Small-cap funds invest in the smaller companies. Micro-cap funds invest in the tiniest of the small companies.

ALERT

You can learn a lot from a mutual fund's name. Sometimes a mutual fund goes crazy with its name. For example, you may run into a fund whose name and investments may be along the lines of XYZ Small-Cap Growth and Income International Asset Allocation fund. This may be a red flag that the fund invests in too small an asset class and that it may be much higher risk than the name hints at. In other words, a simple rule is that a small name usually means that the fund has a much better focus and may be a lower risk proposition. As usual, regardless of the name, there is no substitute for doing your homework before you buy.

Generally, large company funds tend to be less volatile, while mid-cap and small-cap funds tend to be more volatile but offer more opportunity for capital appreciation. As with any investment, profit potential is linked to risk. This is because large companies are established and have a more stable earnings and income stream, while mid-cap and small companies are at different stages of development and have the potential for more bumps along the way. In order to diversify your portfolio, consider investing in all three areas while recognizing the risk/reward ratio and your own risk profile. And as with any other stock-related investment, rising trends will favor most reasonably managed mutual funds, while falling markets will hit most of them, large-cap, mid-cap, and small-cap.

Bond Funds

Bond funds generally have lower risks but also lower returns associated with them than stock funds. Their main function is to provide monthly income to their shareholders. The major advantage of owning a bond fund versus individual bonds is that in a bond fund you get diversification while the fund manager does all the analysis and manages the portfolio. All you have to do is pick a good fund, keep up with how it's doing, make sure that it's meeting your expectations, and gather the income. It's important to remember that bond fund share prices rise and fall; thus, if you own bond funds there is no guarantee that your principal won't rise and fall depending on bond market conditions and their effects on the investment portfolio of the fund. There are primarily three types of bond funds: treasury or government, municipal, and corporate, which includes funds that invest in the high-yield or junk category of bonds.

U.S. Government Bond Funds

These are generally the lowest risk, and thus lowest potential reward, bond funds. Even though the U.S. government runs high deficits, and even though 2013 saw the potential for a debt default in Washington, it didn't happen. And the odds of it happening any time in the next fifty years remains nearly zero. That means that for all intents and purposes, investing in a government bond fund is still relatively safe. These funds, although not exempt from short-term periods of volatility, are excellent vehicles for stable income and for providing an antidote to the potential volatility of the stock fund portion of your portfolio.

ESSENTIAL

It will be interesting to watch the performance of U.S. government bond mutual funds in the next few years. That's because the period of record low interest rates may be coming to an end. As of October 2014, the U.S. Federal Reserve was expected to end its aggressive bond buying program, a likely prelude to a period where the central bank may raise interest rates for an unknown period of time.

Municipal Bond Funds

These are bond funds that invest in intermediate or long-term municipal bonds. Cities, counties, states, and other municipal entities, including school districts, use the proceeds from these bond issuances to finance new road construction or repairs, upgrade sewer systems, or build a new high school. The incentive of most municipal bonds is that investors don't pay federal and often state taxes on the income they receive from the bonds. This extends to municipal bond funds as well. Because the income is not taxed, it tends to be lower than the income you receive from other bonds, though. Municipal bond funds can invest in national, state, or local bonds. These bond funds may be very attractive to investors in high tax states. This advantage may only apply to bond funds that invest in the state itself, though, which is why there are many municipal bond funds that carry the state's name in their title.

Corporate Bond Funds

Corporate bond funds specialize in owning bonds primarily issued by private companies. There are multiple types of corporate bonds, with their quality being based on the kind of corporation that issues them. Generally, good-quality companies with a proven track record issue the highest-rated corporate bonds. As company fundamentals and circumstances decline, so does their credit quality, and the risk of default increases. Ratings agencies have systems to evaluate and rate corporate bonds. Corporate bond fund prospectuses detail the general quality of their holdings. The key term to look for in the prospectus and in the fund literature is "investment grade."

FACT

Socially responsible funds can sometimes be controversial since there is no set definition of the term "socially responsible." In general these funds tend to avoid products that involve animal testing, tobacco, defense companies, and companies that produce guns. Many avoid companies that may be involved with child labor. If you are interested in this kind of investing, you have to read the fund literature carefully and match it with your own criteria. It can be difficult to match socially responsible funds with profit, though, which is the driving force of investing.

These funds balance their risk to you by offering a higher return, but beware of funds that offer significantly higher yields, as they will almost certainly hold large quantities of high-yield or junk bonds with a much higher risk of a default happening and costing you money. Funds that hold large chunks of these bonds are very high risk and are not for everyone.

Mutual Fund Investing Checklist

This chapter has a lot of information about mutual fund investing. Use this comprehensive list as a quick reference when deciding upon your mutual funds:

- Mutual funds are excellent investment vehicles for young and new investors. A good way to understand them is to consider them as indirect ways to invest in certain asset classes.
- Investing in mutual funds takes away one aspect of research, that of finding stocks, bonds, or a good mix of them to own, while reducing the work and effort that managing a portfolio of direct investments requires.
- There is a large variety of mutual funds, and that means there is a mutual fund out there that can meet your criteria and can help you get to your goals.
- Mutual funds reflect the general trends of the assets in which they invest. If you own stocks and the stock market crashes, your fund could register significant losses in the short and long term, depending on how the market reacts and how your fund manager adjusts to the situation.
- Bond funds can help cushion the volatility of a stock portfolio but have their own set of risks. Much of the risk in bonds depends on the overall trend of interest rates, the rate of inflation, and the type of bonds in the portfolio. Generally, mutual funds that invest in U.S. government securities are safer than funds that invest in corporate bonds. Funds that invest in high-yield or junk bonds are the highest risk.
- Past performance is not a guarantee of future performance. Before buying shares in a fund, check to see what a fund has done in up markets and down markets. If possible, check to see what a fund has done in an environment as similar as possible to the one you are experiencing in the present. Remember that a particular fund manager in the past may have

been a superstar with a vision that delivered extraordinary results and that the current fund manager may or may not be in the same category.

- You can invest in balanced or asset allocator mutual funds. Balanced funds invest in a mix of stocks and bonds. Asset allocator funds allocate their resources among different asset classes. This usually includes a mix of stocks, bonds, and cash-equivalent securities.

CHAPTER 11

Combining Funds for Performance

There is a golden rule in investing: If you can't sleep because you're worried about what you own, you shouldn't own it. Nicely, there is a counter rule: If you put together a nice mix of assets, you won't have any trouble sleeping. So while a person can have some fun linking investments and sleep, at the end of the day, literally, how you allocate your mutual fund portfolio is not just directly related to your sleep, but also your pocketbook, your retirement plan, your income goals, and meeting your overall investment goals. This chapter considers how you can combine your risk tolerance and your goals into a mutual fund portfolio that delivers reasonable returns over time and lets you get some sleep.

Your Risk Tolerance

Chapter 1 gave your risk tolerance profile a checkup. So, by this stage of the book, you should have a good idea as to whether you are a conservative, moderate, or aggressive investor. Now, it's time to put your knowledge to work in order to put together a mutual fund portfolio that fits your risk profile and your investment goals.

Once you know your risk tolerance, you can start to put together a mix of funds that, together, will deliver the kinds of returns that you are comfortable with. It is important to remember that although mutual funds do spread out the risk of owning stocks and bonds, they still reflect the risk of the assets that they own. Thus, part of putting together the right mix of funds involves considering how they will perform during difficult markets, and whether your risk tolerance will let you hold them through thick and thin.

ESSENTIAL

Look for the sweet spot. Part of knowing your risk tolerance is recognizing that being conservative will reduce your returns as well as your risk, while being aggressive will increase returns but also increase risks. The key to success is to be aware of this simple principle and to make the mental connection.

While individual stocks can make you a lot of money in the short term, mutual funds tend to deliver their better returns over the long term. This is because an individual stock can respond to earnings or other positive news immediately, while a mutual fund, even if it holds a hot stock, also has other stocks, and sometimes a mixture of assets. So, the hot stock is only a portion of a diversified portfolio and only has a partial effect on the net asset value, or share price of the fund.

It can be difficult to hold on to mutual funds during bad markets. The most important thing is to remain patient and to know that eventually markets turn around. By reviewing the history of how any fund you invest in, whether it is a growth, growth and income, or any other category, does on the rebound after a bad period in the market, you can have an idea as to how things might develop in the future. Where fund investors make mistakes is in picking the wrong fund(s), and then becoming impatient.

ALERT

The prospectus holds many answers that will help you make decisions. A mutual fund prospectus tells the story of what to expect when you buy shares of the fund. Not only will you get the fund's investment philosophy, its asset holdings and allocation, and its overall approach to investing, but you will also get a glimpse into past performance. History isn't everything, but knowing how a fund performs during a bad market is essential if you are planning on holding shares for several years.

Diversification Is Your Friend

When you diversify your fund portfolio, you spread risk around. And successful diversification means owning several different types of mutual funds and allocating them in a way that your risk of a major loss is decreased. Thus, when you own three different aggressive stock funds, you are not diversifying your risk, but most likely increasing it, as you may hold not just the same types of stocks, but you may actually be repeating a fair number of stocks in the three different funds. What that means is that if one of the funds gets hit, because they all own the same type of stock, and often hold many of the same stocks, all three of your aggressive funds will get hit, and you will increase your losses.

Understanding Diversification

The concept is simple: Own mutual funds that invest in different assets or asset classes and spread your risk around. The practice is more difficult, as several key questions arise, such as:

- What is the ideal mix of mutual funds?
- How many mutual funds should you own in order to properly diversify your portfolio?
- How often should you change your asset allocation?

It is by developing a clear, thorough, and concise plan that you answer those questions and begin the process that leads you to the place where you can balance your goals and your risk tolerance in the development of your mutual fund portfolio.

Achieving Diversification

Diversification requires thought and an understanding of the purpose of your portfolio, as the funds you choose will emerge from this exercise. Here are some guidelines:

- **Be clear when setting your investment goals.** This is the step that will both guide you and set the rest of your plan in motion. You can't have enough detail here. Consider your time frame, your risk tolerance, and the purpose of your portfolio, such as long-term growth for retirement, current income, or both.
- **Choose quality over quantity.** Pick one fund at a time. Match the fund to your goal based on whether it fits your investment strategy. If one fund takes care of your goal, then choose that one fund and wait to see how things develop. Evaluate the fund over a few months, perhaps a quarter, and see how things are working out. Consider what kind of market is unfolding and ask yourself how your fund might do if things change. The answer to that question and how it fits into your investment goal will send you in the right direction.
- **Keep it simple.** Don't make this too difficult on yourself. When you've chosen a fund that meets your criteria, don't add a similar fund. For example, most growth funds will trend in a similar way, because they invest in similar stocks. Once you've chosen a fund from a particular category, go on to the next category. If the first fund doesn't work out over a couple of months or a quarter, you may want to switch it for a different fund from the same category.
- **Fewer is better.** If you find that by choosing two or three funds you've met your goals, that's great. There is no need to have more than what you need. For example, if you are a conservative investor and don't want to lose sleep, you may choose a good balanced or asset allocator fund as your only vehicle.
- **Remember to evaluate your goals and your funds' performance.** It's a good rule to look at your funds' performance on at least a weekly basis and to

consider making changes to your portfolio, perhaps on a quarterly basis, if your goals change or if the funds aren't delivering the goods.

Considering Your Choices

Once you've decided your investment goals, and have reconciled them with your risk profile, it's time to find some mutual funds to plug into your portfolio. And while reading a fund's prospectus is worthwhile, it makes sense to have an independent source of information. That's where knowing your way around the World Wide Web comes in handy. Once you've reached the point where you're going to add funds to your portfolio, a great place to centralize your mutual fund research is Morningstar.com (*www.morningstar .com*). This service has both a free and a premium service. The free service is well worth your time. If you think you may want more detail, you can sign up for a fourteen-day free trial.

Choosing a Fund Family

Big is usually, but not always, safe when it comes to choosing a fund family. That's because large, well-established fund families have money, and money tends to attract good management. It is important to understand that "safe" is a relative term. Just because a fund family is large, it doesn't guarantee that their funds will outperform the market, or even mutual funds from smaller fund families. But because the company has been around for a long time, there is a very accessible track record.

For example, Fidelity, Vanguard, and American are huge fund families with gigantic mutual funds that by and large perform in tune with the overall market or sector that they track. In addition, in a tough market, especially one in which you want to sell shares in a fund, or even close an account, it is unlikely that you will encounter any problems in doing so. Size also provides better data, and better security for your money online. For example, during the Heartbleed security threat, Fidelity's website informed its shareholders that the security vulnerability caused by the encryption software that made other websites unsafe wasn't a problem since the company used a totally different technology. The point is that big money families, although not invincible, may have better resources to protect clients from non-investment-related damage than smaller companies.

ALERT

Online investing platforms and mutual fund company websites may have security vulnerabilities. Read the security tab on the website. Ask fund representatives questions about online security. And pay attention to the news with regard to security problems in the financial services industry.

The Fund's Objective

Your first step is to match your goal to the fund's objective. If you want aggressive growth or capital appreciation, make sure the fund's objective states that clearly in its literature and compare the information to what you find in an independent source like Morningstar. If the statement in the prospectus is vague, it means that the fund manager likes to have leeway. Leeway could lead to "drift" from the advertised objective. And while drift can work in your favor, you need to decide whether you can handle it if it turns against you.

Investment Risk

The fund should state its risk profile plainly, and you should be comfortable with the level of risk in the fund if you are going to invest in it. Make sure that the fund's risk and objective match and that the combination of the two is a good match for your risk profile. If a fund is an asset allocator but the prospectus says that it's a high-risk fund, you should probably pass on it even if you are an aggressive investor. Remaining true to the fund category and how it matches your risk profile is your best bet.

Once you've made sure that the fund says what it does and actually does what it says, it's important to know how the fund performs in up markets, in down markets, and in relationship to the S&P 500 or its benchmark index, and how it stacks up to its competition over time. If your account is with a single mutual fund company, see if there is more than one fund in the stable that invests in the category. If there is, choose the one that has the better performance over time and that meets your risk profile and expectations.

Breakdown of Investments

The prospectus should clearly list the limits of the fund's investment breakdown. For example, it should note if the fund's maximum exposure to stocks is 60% or a different figure, as well as its maximum bond exposure. The fund should also tell you whether it uses leverage or margin, investing with borrowed money, or if it sells securities short, the practice of borrowing securities in the hope that they fall in price in order to profit from the price decline. If a fund relies on margin, leverage, derivatives, and short selling for a large portion of its activity, it is not a good bet for a beginning investor.

Financial History

A fund should also list its history, preferably for the life of the fund, but for no less than ten years. This information should be detailed on a per share basis and should include year-by-year details on net asset values, dividends, and total returns so that you can gauge performance on an annual basis. This history should also include details on the fund's expenses and fees and the kind of holdings the fund has had over time.

Parsing Past Performance

The financial world's signature disclosure statement and disclaimer is: "past performance is no guarantee of future performance." The reason is that things change and change can affect a fund's performance. Aside from the economy, interest rates, and other external factors, such as politics, mutual fund performance may be affected by sector and industry trends, which can lead to one or two great years of good performance followed by several years of mediocre growth or decline in the net asset value. More importantly, the reversal of any of these factors, which may have held performance down for the past three to four years, could be the verge of a price reversal for any mutual fund. For that reason, the best way to look at past performance is in the context of the present with regard to all pertinent factors, including the fund's current holdings.

Also review what the fund's category has done through any significant period of the market and compare it to the fund's performance during the same period. If a small-cap fund didn't do well when small-caps weren't doing well, such as during the decade of the 1990s, it's not the fund; it's more likely the times that held it back. By the same token, if a small-cap fund delivered stellar returns during the same period, it may be worth looking into it, as it could be a sign of superior stock picking by the manager.

Finally, when looking at long-term performance, consider the effect of fees, operating expenses, and sales charges. Have your CPA look at the tax consequences of the fund's annual payouts. This does not apply to shares held in an IRA or other retirement account. Also consider the size of the fund. The larger the fund, the harder it is for the manager to deploy his cash in the markets, given the need for very large share blocks. Pay attention to how long the current manager has been running the fund. If the fund has an excellent ten-year performance record, but the current manager started six months ago, the ten-year performance record is essentially meaningless.

FACT

When you sell shares of mutual funds in the same family, it's called an exchange. If you do it by phone, just tell the representative that you would like to exchange shares from Fund A to Fund B. If you are making the exchange online, just follow the directions on the website. The exchange will take place at the closing price at 4:00 P.M. EST on the day you make the decision, unless you make the exchange after hours. Then it will be made at the closing price on the next business day.

How Long Should You Hold Mutual Fund Shares?

Ideally, your time frame for holding a mutual fund should be one to five years. But there are some things to consider before you make your decision with regard to the holding period. For example:

- Understand where you are in the market cycle. If you buy a stock mutual fund in the fifth year of a raging bull market, you should expect that some kind of pullback or extended period of flat prices will develop in the next few weeks or perhaps months after you buy your shares. In this case, you may want to wait until an opportunity for lower prices materializes, or to buy small numbers of shares over time as the market cycle unfolds. If stocks have been falling for the past twelve to eighteen months, the odds of some kind of rally are higher than normal. This might be a good time to buy some shares and see what happens.

- Know what kind of fund you are investing in. If after looking at the market cycle, you get worried about losing money in a market correction, but you still want to put some money in a fund, consider a bond fund or an asset allocator fund. These tend to move more slowly than the stock market and are more likely to produce smaller damage to your principal.
- If you think you've made a mistake, exchange the shares into your money market fund and wait to see what happens next. There is no reason for you to agonize over taking big losses just to prove a point.

Six Fund Investment Strategies

Mutual fund investing can be confusing. But it doesn't have to be if you follow some simple rules that will keep you on the right side of things.

Start Now

Time is your best friend. The earlier you get started, the better. But don't be put off because you don't think that you have enough time to meet your goals. Even if you make your first investment in two months, by starting the process now, you will be ready sooner than if you wait. The data is clear: compounding works over time. And there is no time like now.

Go Big

Invest as much money as you possibly can as early as possible. This does not mean that you should throw your money at anything. But if you put as sizable a quantity of money as possible in a money market fund now, it will be available for you when you find the right fund.

Information Is Salvation

The more you know about your investments, the better off you'll be and the fewer will be your chances of taking big losses. Know as much as you can about your mutual fund and the securities, stocks, bonds, and other asset classes that it holds. As you learn, you will gain confidence and experience, which will lead to better financial decisions.

Stay Aggressive

Aggressiveness pays off in the early stages of your investing career, when tempered by the knowledge that time is on your side. That means that putting money in growth-oriented mutual funds is a must in your early years. As you get closer to retirement, you can start scaling back. Being aggressive does not mean that you should be foolhardy. Prudent investors know that growth is part of a balanced, well-diversified portfolio. It is in this context that aggressive growth funds should be used.

Keep the Money Working

Keep your investment money in your investment portfolio if at all possible. If you take money out of your investment portfolio every time you have a financial emergency, you are taking money away from your future. Although this is difficult, it's a must to avoid the temptation of dipping into your investments to pay bills if at all possible. Before doing so, try every other way of taking care of any financial surprise.

Watch the Market

External events can hit your mutual funds hard. That means that you have to watch your own portfolio. Don't trust your portfolio manager to do anything other than what his job requires. If the market starts to look dicey, it makes sense to put any new money in the safety of your money market fund and wait to see what the market does before putting new money into your stock funds. Use the same basic strategy for your bond funds. Sometimes building up some extra cash makes sense, especially if you're looking to put it to work later at lower prices.

Tracking Your Funds' Performance

Once you become an active mutual fund shareholder, it's important to keep up with your fund's activity. Start by reviewing your mutual fund order on the confirmation slip that you will receive, either by mail or e-mail. Make sure that your order was put in correctly. Check the amount of money you invested and verify that you got the correct number of shares. Pay special attention to any fees that were deducted when you bought the shares, especially if the fund is advertised as a no-load fund, and inquire about any discrepancies that you perceive as soon as you notice them. If you buy the fund online, you should see a confirmation page before putting the order through. If you are buying the fund on the phone, your mutual fund company representative should confirm the order to you before putting it through. Still, make it a habit to review your order confirmations as soon as possible after you receive them in the mail and compare them to your wishes.

ESSENTIAL

The most cost-effective way to buy mutual funds is through an online discount brokerage account. Even more effective is opening the account with a big mutual fund company that offers brokerage accounts as well. Then you can exchange between the funds in the broker's family or buy funds in other families, usually with a lower commission than what you would get from a full-service broker.

Check your funds' performances at least on a quarterly basis. In the past, it was not unusual to check mutual funds once or twice a year. But in the age of high frequency trading, a volatile world, and an economy that has recovered sluggishly from a near depression in 2008, more frequent checks are a good idea. Make it a habit to compare your fund to its benchmark index and to other funds in its category. Check on the fees charged by competing funds and fund families and make changes if they make sense.

When to Sell

The most difficult decision in investing is when to sell. But it doesn't have to be difficult. That's because with a good plan you've decided when to sell, before you buy. Generally, you should sell a fund when it no longer fits with your long-term plans. Some reasons that can contribute to this are poor performance, a change in the fund's management, bad service from the fund's family, or even market conditions. Also consider selling if your fund isn't meeting expectations or keeping up with the market or its category. If you see that most funds in the category aren't doing well, you should consider avoiding the entire category of funds and rethink your strategy and goals.

Mostly, you should sell your fund if holding it is making you uncomfortable. Maybe it's too volatile and you're starting to get nervous. If you're reaching for the antacids, that's a sure sign that you need to look elsewhere. Your best move will be never coming back to the same fund again.

The Fund Monitoring Checklist

Here are nine tips that will keep you from losing sleep over your mutual funds:

- Inspect and carefully verify every document you receive regarding your investments. If you find errors, address them immediately and record responses and corrections in writing.
- Keep notes of all conversations with investment professionals, ranging from your CPA and financial advisor to mutual fund or brokerage company reps, with regard to your portfolio.
- Make sure that all investment-related correspondence is addressed to you. Your advisor should get copies. You get the first copy.
- Keep up with your paperwork. If you make a trade and you don't get confirmation by e-mail or regular mail within a reasonable amount of time, find out why.
- If something unfamiliar or unexpected shows up in your account, contact your fund company or brokerage right away.
- Never make your investment checks to an individual. Always make them to the company and list your account number. Brokerage companies

and mutual fund companies always provide investment slips with critical ID information that you should include with your check.

- If you decide to use a broker, make sure you meet her in her office before putting down any money.
- Know your investments. Don't rely on someone else's research or sales pitch. Do your own homework. Get used to good independent websites like *www.finance.yahoo.com* where you can find great deals of information free of charge.
- When in doubt, review your portfolio. There is no reason, just because you have mutual funds, that you shouldn't keep up with what's going on. The *Wall Street Journal, Investor's Business Daily*, and *Barron's* are great sources of information that can help you put your investments in their proper perspective.

The bottom line is that mutual funds are great investment vehicles for beginners and experienced investors. But just because the fund manager is making the buy and sell decisions, that shouldn't be a reason for you not to be informed and involved.

CHAPTER 12

Exchange Traded Mutual Funds: The New Frontier

As mutual funds became popular, the restrictions on the number of exchanges placed on fund shares as well as the increase in the market's volatility created difficulties for some investors. Over time, especially during down markets, it became clear that a new asset class that combined the properties of stocks and mutual funds was needed. So in the 1990s the first exchange traded mutual fund (ETF) was created. And the rest, as they say, is history. ETFs have revolutionized the way both individual and professional investors put their money to work in the markets. This chapter is all about how you can make ETFs work for you and how to avoid the potential errors that can cost you money.

What Are ETFs?

Think of an ETF as a hybrid, part stock and part mutual fund. The stock part comes from the fact that ETFs trade like stocks, on an open exchange, through a brokerage account that charges a commission for the ETF. The mutual fund part is that ETFs, like the traditional mutual fund, are a portfolio. So when you buy an ETF, you are buying shares in the portfolio, but because it trades like a stock, you don't have to wait until the market closes to own the shares.

There are over 1,300 ETFs with $1.7 trillion in assets. Eighty-five percent (85%) of those assets are in equity-related funds and 14% are in bond funds. The remaining 1% of assets resides in hybrid funds, which hold multiple kinds of assets. And although this is a growing asset class, compared to mutual funds, of which there are nearly 10,000, it's still a relatively small group. Nevertheless, ETFs are important and may make sense as part of your portfolio. Here are several facts to help you know why:

- ETFs are well suited for short- to intermediate-term trading. You may not be interested in trading when you are a beginner. But as you become more experienced, trading may become attractive. ETFs are ideal for this kind of investing because, like mutual funds, you are investing in an index or a sector. Thus, you don't have to pick stocks. When you buy an ETF, you are picking a trend; thus, the analysis required is less tedious, but still offers you excellent profit potential if you know what you are looking for.

- There are no trading limits on ETFs. While mutual fund companies limit the number of times you can exchange in and out of a fund, you can trade ETFs like you trade stocks. And you can use margin, which opens up your ability for short-term trading opportunities.

- There are ETFs that offer you the opportunity to sell the market, or specific sectors, short. While this is risky and is not recommended for beginners, short selling is a useful skill when you want to hedge your risk to protect your portfolio, or when you see a sector of the market that is weak.

- ETFs offer built-in leverage. As with short selling, the use of leverage is dangerous even for experienced investors. Yet, it may have a place in your strategy at some point when you become experienced. By using leverage, some ETFs move at two or three times the rate of their underlying index. This kind of investing is to be avoided by beginners.

- ETFs may offer you better tax treatment and fee structures than mutual funds.

ETFs Versus Mutual Funds

There are many differences between mutual funds and ETFs. The biggest three are: since ETFs trade on an exchange like stocks, you can trade them at any time during the trading day; there is no minimum or limit in the number of ETF shares you can buy; and each and every time you buy ETF shares, you will have to pay a brokerage commission. ETF management fees tend to be lower than mutual fund fees, but that is something that you should check out before you trade any ETF shares.

ALERT

Some ETFs are leveraged, which means that they move at two or three times the speed of the underlying asset. The ETF's literature will plainly explain the amount of leverage in the fund. For example, if you own an S&P 500 index that is leveraged to trade at twice the range of the index, and the index moved 1% on any given day, the ETF would move 2% on that day. That's great when the market rises but not good on a down day. Consider what would happen to your portfolio if the market lost 5% of its value in one day due to some awful external event. Leverage is best left to experienced investors and professionals.

Perhaps the biggest difference, and one that could make a big difference, is that ETFs don't make capital gain distributions like mutual funds. ETFs, especially ETFs that invest in bonds, do pay dividends that may be taxable. Remember, a capital gain distribution, in the context of mutual funds, is a different entity than a dividend because capital gains are incurred by mutual funds when they sell assets on which they have a profit. A dividend, in the context of a mutual fund, is a pass through of dividend income that the fund has received. On the other hand, ETF shares will incur applicable capital gain taxes when you sell them. Finally, ETFs update their holdings daily on their company website. This is a better deal than what you get with mutual funds, which are only required to report their holdings twice a year. This is important because knowing what you're buying in real time may influence your decision and could save you money in the long run as you avoid investing in something that you may not want.

What Kinds of Investments Can You Make Through ETFs?

As with mutual funds, you can find just about any category of stock or bond represented in an ETF. Historically, stock index ETFs that focused on the popular indexes, such as the S&P 500 and the Dow Jones Industrial Average, were the rage. And this is still the most popular category given their low cost and their ability to track their respective indexes. But as the market has expanded, so have the number of offerings. Now you can buy and sell ETFs that only invest in indexes that focus on aggressive growth or dividend stocks, small stocks, large-cap stocks, or blue chips.

ALERT

Actively managed mutual funds can have higher fees than index ETFs and even some mutual funds. And the return isn't guaranteed to be better since managers can have hot and cold streaks. Also, be aware of the fact that one of the reasons mutual fund companies offer these actively managed ETFs is both to broaden their investor base as well as to increase their fees. In fact, a fair portion of the time actively managed ETFs are basically clones of their traditional mutual fund brethren, often having the identical name. Why pay more for the same assets and sometimes worse performance?

You can also invest in municipal, government, and corporate bond ETFs that hold bonds in durations from short-term to twenty years. ETFs that specialize in real estate investment trusts and preferred stocks are easy to find. You can also trade ETFs that invest in foreign currencies or the U.S.

dollar, and others offer you the opportunity to sell the bond or stock market short, and profit when prices fall. And recently, actively managed ETFs have emerged. These funds, unlike index-based ETFs, use a portfolio manager to make changes in the portfolio based on his indicators and trading philosophy.

As of April 2014, there are only eighty-four actively managed ETFs in existence with $15 billion under management, very low numbers compared to the number of index funds. Surprisingly, actively managed bond funds outnumber their equity brethren.

Animal Crackers and Geometry: Spiders, Vipers, Diamonds, and Cubes

ETFs have great nicknames. But don't let the fun and games distract you from what you are looking for. These are all serious investments and a wrong choice could cost you money.

- **"Spiders"** is the market's nickname for the first family of ETFs, the S&P 500 SPDR ETF (S&P 500 Depository Receipts, NYSE: SPY). This ETF, created by State Street Global Advisors, then spawned the Select Sector SPDRs, which are the first sector-specific ETFs and feature ETFs such as the SPDR Select Sector Fund – Technology (NYSE: XLK) and the Health Care Select Sector SPDR Fund (NYSE: XLV).

- **Diamonds** let you own the stocks of the Dow Jones Industrial Average, while **VIPERs** (Vanguard Index Participation Equity Receipts) are Vanguard-issued ETFs. VIPERs, depending on which one(s) you choose, offer investment opportunities in stocks, bonds, and international markets.

- PowerShares made its mark with the **Cubes** (NYSE: QQQ), the ETF that tracks the Nasdaq 100 Index (which houses the largest capitalization shares in the Nasdaq). By investing in the Cubes, you buy into shares of companies like Google, Microsoft, Apple, and Intel, among others. PowerShares uses a method called "dynamic indexing," which allows them to focus on the best performers in the underlying index.

Mixing ETFs Into Your Portfolio

ETFs can be helpful for diversification or can be used as the only components of a well-structured portfolio. Because of the broad choices in categories and individual funds, your portfolio can participate in a piece of just about every asset category that's available. Perhaps the largest advantage is the fact that you can do this for a lot less than what it would cost you if you bought individual stocks. For example, you could own a large-cap, a mid-cap, and a small-cap index ETF. You can add one, two, or more bond ETFs, coupled with a diversified commodity ETF, a gold ETF, and a real estate investment trust ETF. And you could further diversify your holdings by adding international equity and bond funds. You can mix actively managed mutual funds and ETFs into your portfolio as well, further diversifying your holdings.

FACT

The largest ETF issuer is Barclays, with its iShares. These ETFs cover the entire gamut of investing by offering funds that invest in stocks, bonds, and currencies in most markets of the world.

Choosing Wisely

Choosing which ETFs make sense for your portfolio is similar to how you choose mutual funds or stocks. Take inventory of your situation. Review your financial plan. Consider your short-, intermediate-, and long-term goals, your current holdings, and your risk profile. The answer should be evident once you go through these important and necessary steps.

ALERT

ETFs are ideal for trading. This is because, as a more experienced investor, you will likely develop a better sense of the overall market's trend and ETFs, by design, are trend-following investment vehicles. By using ETFs you can focus on trading the trend instead of individual stocks.

Next, you should consider expenses. Compare any potential ETF to similar mutual funds and review the expenses for each of them, while weighing performance. Index ETFs and traditional funds that invest in similar holdings should perform similarly. But if one is more expensive than the other, your overall returns, especially over the long term, could be affected. Remember that a no-load mutual fund won't charge you commission when you trade, while adding shares to an ETF will carry commission costs every time you buy. In other words, if you find a no-load mutual fund with equal or better performance compared to an ETF, choose the mutual fund. Also important is the cost. A mutual fund may cost less on a per share basis.

Because there is increased competition between ETF families, similar funds from different issuers could have significantly different fees. For example, if Vanguard's S&P 500 ETF has lower fees than the SPDR fund, it might make sense to buy the Vanguard fund, given that it is investing in the same equities and that performance should be nearly identical.

Avoid thinly traded ETFs. Before buying shares, make sure that any ETF has enough capital invested in it and that it is actively traded. If an ETF has assets of more than $10 million and it has a robust trading volume, it makes sense to consider it. If the ETF has less than $10 million and trading volume is less than a few million shares per day, it means that it is not very liquid. And that means that you may have a difficult time when trying to sell shares.

Recognizing Special Situations

There is such a thing as over-diversification. Many investors err by looking for such a high level of variety in their portfolio that they won't miss any kind of move in any market. The truth is that for many investors, less is more. So, before you get yourself into an unmanageable alphabet soup of ETFs and traditional mutual funds, consider your goals and think about how you can get there by keeping things as simple as possible while still giving yourself the opportunity to be flexible and profit from special opportunities.

If your goal is retirement in thirty years, and you are just getting started, there is no point in micromanaging your portfolio. Your first move is to get started. That means that by just fulfilling your asset allocation goals, based on your risk profile, your overall goal, and your time frame, you are on your way. Does this mean that you don't make changes or improve your asset allocation? Of course not; flexibility and the ability to recognize important changes in market dynamics is paramount for your long-term success as an investor.

ALERT

Sector-specific ETFs may be useful in special market situations. For example, if there is a great deal of money that is being invested in energy related stocks, it may make sense to evaluate and consider investing in an energy specific-sector ETF.

For example, if your current core asset allocation consists of a large-cap, a mid-cap, and a small-cap equity ETF along with a diversified bond ETF and you notice that the technology stocks are on a momentum run, it might make sense to add a technology ETF to the mix. Just keep in mind that technology stocks won't go up forever, and these ETFs may not be in your portfolio as long as your core holdings because you may want to sell them if they start to perform badly. In other words, consider carving out special niches inside your portfolio for special situations that can work alongside your core investments. Work this out on paper before you put your money down. Ask yourself questions and develop an analytical routine. By spending a couple of hours per week reviewing the markets and thinking about potential opportunities with a shorter-term time horizon, you may save yourself a lot of trouble later.

Buying and Selling ETFs

If you can trade stocks, you can trade ETFs. The only difference is that with an ETF you get an indexed or a diversified portfolio instead of an individual stock. Otherwise there is no change. You still need a broker. You will pay commission. And before you make the transaction, you need to go down your checklist. Consult your plan. Do your research. Consider when you will sell the shares. And understand the tax implications, if there are any. Just like with stocks, you can add conditions to your trading orders. That means you can use limit orders and sell stops. Here is the big difference, though: If you decide that you made a mistake, you can sell all the shares at any time without getting a notice from your mutual fund company because you sold your shares too soon and they don't want a "day trader" using their funds.

Market Timing with ETFs

Market timing is controversial, and it's difficult to do. And while most investment advisors will tell you it is impossible to time the markets, the fact is that the statement is simply not true. The truth is that market timing is possible, but it is hard work, very risky, and in many ways, it is similar to gambling, which is why most market timers rely on "systems," which are comprised of combinations of indicators and require frequent revision and analysis. Yet, because of their indexed nature and their ease of trading, ETFs are the perfect vehicle for this kind of trading, in which, based on your time frame, it is possible to profit over a few days, a few weeks, or a few months, depending on how long any market trend lasts and how good your timing strategies and attention to detail are.

It's a Risky Business

Market timing is high-risk trading. It's not investing. And it is not something that should be done by investors who are just starting out. But it is something that any investor, who is inclined to take risks, can learn to do, as long as he is aware that the practice can lead to large losses and that it is subject to both winning and losing streaks.

Here is why ETFs are great vehicles for market timing. The only thing that matters to market timers is the trend, the direction of prices. Traders don't care much about the fundamentals. The only thing that matters is whether a market is primarily rising or falling. When you buy stocks, you should pay attention to valuations, management, the company's product cycle, and a host of other parameters that are detailed in Chapters 4–6. Market timing is all about timing the direction of the total market, or a sector of the market. To market timers, the fundamentals are secondary, because they believe that prices reflect the fundamentals. As a result, market timers believe that when the fundamentals change, the direction of prices will also change.

ESSENTIAL

Index specific mutual funds are ideal for market timing. If you know that the largest money flows are going into the S&P 500 index, your best bet, as a market timer, is likely to be to invest in the S&P SPDR (SPY) ETF. This would be a trading decision that would be based on a technical assessment of the market's trend and would require a good working knowledge and comfort level of trend analysis.

Tools of ETF Timing

In order to make their buy and sell decisions, market timers use technical analysis, the study of price charts and trends, to pick entry and exit points for their trades. For example, when the stock market is rising, market timers often buy an index ETF such as the S&P 500 SPDR ETF. The goal of market timing is to remain in any position, such as an ETF, as long as the direction of prices remains intact.

While long-term investors have time on their side, timers are looking to make money over shorter periods of time. That means that they make buy and sell decisions more frequently, sometimes as often as every few days, although most timers are hoping to be in position for at least a few weeks, since the longer the price trend remains intact, the greater the chance for profits. By using price charts and related indicators, timers take away the emotion associated with buying and selling.

Leveraged ETFs and Market Timing

Aggressive traders and market timers often buy a leveraged version of the ETF, which moves at twice or three times the underlying price of the real S&P 500. When they use leverage, market timers can make or lose more money in shorter periods of time. Because market timers hope to turn a sizable profit in a shorter period of time than short-term investors, and because market timers tend to be experienced traders, they can afford to take the added risk of using a leveraged ETF. If a market timer concludes that the stock market is about to fall, she may buy shares in an ETF that sells the S&P 500 index short. These specialized ETFs, also known as inverse ETFs, rise in price when the S&P 500 falls.

Timing Beyond Stock ETFs

Because there are ETFs for all markets, market timers can use ETFs to time bonds and other investment classes. For example, you can use ETFs to trade commodities, including gold, oil, and agricultural commodities such as coffee, wheat, corn, and even cattle. There are specialized ETFs that offer the opportunity to trade in these areas either as part of a commodity index or as separate commodities. Market timers can also time currencies such as the euro, the Japanese yen, the British pound, the Swiss franc, the U.S. dollar, and the Canadian and Australian currencies. And yes, there are leveraged and inverse ETFs available for timing markets beyond stocks.

ETFs as Hedging Instruments

Hedging is the practice of investing in a financial instrument that limits the risk of another instrument. A common hedge is the use of bonds or bond funds to limit the risk in a stock portfolio. Experienced traders and investors use ETFs as hedging instruments. Aside from using bond ETFs, traders also use inverse ETFs to hedge risk. For example, let's say that the stock market has risen 10%–15% in a few weeks. History shows that this kind of an advance is not just rare, but likely unsustainable. In such a scenario, rather than selling a portfolio, an experienced trader may buy shares in an inverse S&P 500 ETF with the hopes that if the stock market corrects, his losses will be less as the inverse fund shares will rise in price. This trading technique, as with other market timing techniques, is not without risk but could become useful as you gain experience.

Tracking Your ETFs

Tracking your ETFs is just like tracking your stocks. You can find daily prices in the *Wall Street Journal*, *Investor's Business Daily*, Yahoo! Finance, and many other sources, including your ETF family's webpage or your online brokerage account, which will give you tick-by-tick prices if you like that kind of real-time information.

All you need to know is your trading symbols. Price tables will usually include price changes and percentage changes, as well as providing fifty-two-week price ranges. Some will provide dividend payment dates and dividend yield information. *Investor's Business Daily* has one of the most complete ETF sections in the market and may be worth subscribing to just for that.

CHAPTER 13

Green Investing

If you're the type of person that takes reusable bags to the grocery store, likes to eat organic foods, and rides a bicycle whenever possible instead of driving a car, environmentally responsible investing may be for you. Believe it or not, there are growing ways to invest in this general and fairly recent new trend, which can be useful, not just for your pocketbook, but also for the environment.

What Are Green Investments?

The green investment trend has been unfolding for several years. It is in fact becoming, to a fairly large degree, part of the normal environment. But that does not mean that it should be seen in a different light. There is a fair amount of socially responsible potential still left in it, and there are some pitfalls. Generally, political causes and investments don't mix well. That's because investments are about making money, and political causes are about bringing about change. Green investing is no different in this regard. And yes, there is still a fair amount of gap bridging left to accomplish. But there are some areas of this sector where you can have your organic cake, eat it, and make some money. That's what this chapter is about: finding the areas where environmental green and the green of profit meet.

A true green company is one that puts its money behind helping the environment via practices that decrease pollution and conserve natural resources and, through its business practices, actively attempts to help the environment. A true green company doesn't just curb its existing practices that could harm the environment. It actively pursues the improvement of the environment. This is a significant distinction, because green investors monitor this dynamic and actually move their money away from companies who don't fulfill this one important criterion.

As a result, Wall Street and Main Street are paying closer attention to the trend and making changes, expanding investment choices in the area. There are indexes that track green companies, and mutual funds and ETFs that invest in these companies, making it easier for individual investors to participate. Just as important, for income investors, is the fact that municipalities and corporations are also selling bonds to finance environmentally friendly projects. Finally, as you learn more about companies through your investment research, you might find ways to change your behavior as a consumer. The key is to carefully research the general trends in the sector, and then to become acquainted with further detail as you prepare to make investment decisions.

Green Stocks

Green stocks let you become part owner of a company whose efforts, in delivering its goods and services, are positive for the environment. This may be achieved by their use of cleaner fuels, or by their development of new methods that produce less, or cleaner, waste products. Sometimes these companies are donors of capital or volunteer their employees for socially responsible and environmentally positive causes.

FACT

You don't need to reinvent the wheel or look for a company that proposes to fuel the world's energy needs with moon rock dust to be a green investor. You can be "green" and use your common sense. Whole Foods Market (Nasdaq: WFM) and Starbucks (Nasdaq: SBUX) are examples of green companies that are well integrated into the mainstream. Both are leaders in their industrial sectors. And both do more than many companies to walk the "green" walk by using solar power to fuel stores, buying products from local organic farmers, and by giving portions of their profits to green causes such as clean water initiatives.

As with any kind of socially responsible or "cause" investing, there is the potential for fraud. Here is a set of questions that can help you make better decisions:

- Does the corporation that you might invest in actually have products, or are things still in the development stage?
- Is there a reasonable time frame to test the products and market them?
- What is the market that the company is targeting? Is there actually a need or even a niche for the product?
- Is the company speaking in exact, real market terms? Or are they just describing generalities without any specifics?
- Does the company describe how it expects its products to evolve and how it will expand its market share over time?

- How does this corporation's ideas, technology and business models, management team, and practices compare to others who are leaders in the sector?

If you can't get good, solid answers to these questions, especially when you are looking through company-produced documents, it might be best if you look somewhere else for a place to put your hard-earned green.

Green Bonds

A green bond is a financial instrument, issued by a corporation or a municipality, where the proceeds will be used to finance an environmentally related project. Unlike traditional loans, where a borrower asks for money from a bank, bonds are loans that spread the risk by using money borrowed from the public, investors, and other entities, including banks. For you, as an investor, bonds let you participate in income-producing opportunities.

If the issuer is a corporation, you should consider the default risk along with your green meter, using the six questions outlined in the previous section. Corporate bonds are rated by Standard & Poor's, Moody's, and other rating agencies. Lower-rated bonds pay a higher interest rate. Depending on the rating and the interest rate, you can decide whether you want to take the risk. Remember that a high interest rate is often a sign that the company is desperate and that there is a fairly good risk of default.

Green loans issued by municipalities are also rated by S&P and Moody's. Because they are municipal bonds, though, the interest that you receive will not likely be taxed by the federal government or, in most cases, by the state government. This will likely make them more attractive, especially if you are not using them in a tax-deferred retirement account. As with corporate bonds, if the interest rate seems to be well above the norm, do your homework about the municipality issuing the bond.

Official green bonds (Qualified Green Building and Sustainable Design Project Bonds) are tax-exempt bonds issued both by corporations and municipalities. They earn this moniker because the federal government designates them for the purpose of developing underdeveloped, underutilized land parcels or old abandoned buildings. Often, the land where the work is to be done is polluted and contaminated, and the bond proceeds are used to clean up the environmental problems.

Green Funds

You can find traditional mutual funds or exchange traded mutual funds (ETFs) that specialize in green companies. ETFs may be a better deal because you can look at their component stocks in real time and apply the green meter to the companies in the ETF in real time. Traditional mutual funds only publish their holdings periodically, often just once per year. Just because a fund says that it's green, it may not be totally green. Remember, when you read the prospectus pay close attention to how much leeway the manager has to pick the fund's holdings. If the prospectus tells you that the fund may invest its money, "as much as 50%" or something along those lines, in green companies, it may not be for you.

ESSENTIAL

It's good to find a list where you may find a lot of green ETFs to consider. One such list can be found at Kapitall Wire (*http://wire.kapitall .com/investment-idea/a-list-of-green-etfs-for-responsible-investing*), a service that looks for hot trends in the market. Aside from listing a representative sample of ETFs that market themselves as "green," the page also gives you the option to "dig deeper" into the stocks inside the ETFs.

Green funds come in three basic varieties: eco-friendly, alternative energy, and sustainable resource funds.

Eco-Friendly Funds

This is the broadest category of green funds, as the fund managers can invest in companies that strive to improve the environment, produce and design environmentally friendly products, or engage in activities that are aimed at reducing their negative impact on the environment.

The Calvert family of mutual funds (*www.calvert.com*) specializes in green mutual funds, and has a variety of offerings. The Calvert Large-Cap fund may strike a good balance for you. The fund specializes in corporations that are environmentally friendly but have also found the sweet spot in delivering profits to their shareholders.

As a general rule, beware of false claims or mushy language in fund prospectuses and other information. Look at the holdings of the fund before buying shares. If you are truly committed to green investing, you don't want to put your money in the wrong place.

Alternative Energy Funds

These funds invest in companies that develop or produce alternative or renewable energy sources, such as solar and wind power, biofuels, or hydroelectric power, and the companies that are involved in the infrastructure and manufacturing of the components used to make the final products used in alternative fuel production. An example of such a fund is the First Trust ISE Global Wind Energy ETF (NYSE: FAN). Here is the type of analysis that you should consider when looking at this ETF. According to a Morningstar .com search, in May of 2014, FAN's asset allocation was composed of 57% in utilities and 38% in industrial companies. The rest of the holdings (5%) were in the energy consumer cyclical and basic materials companies.

FACT

Dig beneath the surface in order to grow your cache of ideas and your knowledge base. Looking inside the holdings of an ETF should lead you to do research on individual companies whose stock may be worth owning, on their own or along with the ETF. For example, the largest holding of any ETF could provide you with clues as to what kind of new trends may be unfolding in any particular sector. It makes sense to jot these companies down and do more research on them later.

FAN's largest holding in May 2014 was Vestas Wind Systems, a Danish company that is the world's number one manufacturer of wind turbines. The rest of the top five holdings included a Spanish company also involved in the manufacturing of wind turbines, a utility that distributes natural gas and electricity generated by wind power, and a power generating plant construction company. This ETF is clearly an example of a green fund, based on the best information available online.

Sustainable Resource Funds

Sustainable resource funds invest in companies that share the double goal of maximizing profits without depleting natural resources. This is where the water funds fit. These funds invest in the entire gamut of the water industry, including water distribution, water consumption, and other subsectors of the water industry. The water industry is widely tracked by multiple indexes, and in turn, there are several ETFs and mutual funds that in turn track individual indexes. A diversified global water ETF is the Guggenheim S&P Global Water Index ETF (ARCX: CGW). Non-exchange traded water funds are available, too, such as the actively managed Calvert Global Water Fund (CFWAX).

Looking Beyond the Green

Green investing is appealing. After all, you can make money while helping the environment. It sounds great, doesn't it? In reality, though, green investing can be just as dangerous as mainstream investing, and often for the same reasons. As with any investment, when the premise, the investment vehicle, and the execution of the management team at a company or a mutual fund are what they say they are, and everyone does what they say they will, the odds are in your favor. But scam artists are everywhere. And because green investing is a good cause, the unscrupulous are attracted to the sector like flies on waste.

It's not just midnight infomercials crafted by con artists that will try to fool you. Because green means money, big Madison Avenue advertising firms craft green "messaging" statements and "narratives" for their clients, in order to paint companies that aren't green with the benevolent shade in order to sell more products. The attraction of the green trend is so large and the "messaging" is so widespread that a new term, "greenwashing," has emerged. That's where companies, much like politicians, try to "spin" their products and practices to make them look green, when in fact, close scrutiny often leads to finding out that there is more effort on the spin than on the green practices advertised.

ALERT

Beware of haughty promises when it comes to green investing. Dishonest people will try to fool you on a regular basis. When it comes to green investing, stick to well-vetted companies, ETFs, and mutual funds with established track records and you will give yourself the best chance of making money. Check out helpful information at Good Money (*www.goodmoney.com*), The Forum for Sustainable and Responsible Investment (*www.ussif.org*), and SocialFunds (*www.social funds.com*).

How can you see through the not-so-green fog? Use your common sense. If it seems foul, it probably is. If it seems sensible, question it anyway. Look deeply into what companies do to create the "green" effect. Ask tough questions. Is a biofuel company using twice the amount of oil for input in order to create clean fuels, thus negating the positive environmental effect? Do agricultural companies burn land, creating smoke pollution, in order to plant biofuel stock? Do their biofuels actually pollute the air more than gasoline? (Some forms of ethanol do.) What happens to a riverbed and a fish population if you remove that algae to craft synthetic motor oil? The river could die, creating a waste area and a breeding ground for disease, not to mention that the water supply for a large stretch of farmland might be harmed. And if the "green" idea is so good, then why is it still in the development stage after ten years? If you look hard enough, you will find that in many cases the "green" outcome is achieved at the price of lots of environmental destruction and harm, and that the long-term implications may be worse than going to the corner gas station and filling up your SUV. Also, try to keep the searching balanced. The green activists are not exempt from their own spin. That's life these days. Everyone has an agenda and everyone is willing to craft an effective "narrative" to win.

Does this mean that "green" is bad? No way. Green investing and green initiatives have huge positive potential for the environment, and for profits. The take-home message, though, is that as an investor, you need to become an investigative reporter and dig for the best answers possible before putting your money into something that may cost you.

Your Green Portfolio

Green investing has come a long way since the twentieth century. Companies that are sincere and well managed are flourishing as they find balance between environmental consciousness and profit. And investors who used to ignore the trend are having a second look. From a price performance standpoint, big money players are the ones that move stocks and bonds. So, when a nongreen mutual fund sees something in a green company, it is quite likely that the stock of the company is going to move higher. As an investor, you need to be aware of this dynamic, and you need to be able to act on it because as money comes into the sector, your odds of profiting also rise.

Adapt the basic tenets of investing to the green sector and you will be well served. Know your risk profile. Look for leaders in the field. Seek out top management teams that clearly state their objectives and execute their plans efficiently and successfully. Keep up with the general trends of the sector, look for news on companies that you own, and monitor how a company responds to the news. Put together a good watch list of ETFs and mutual funds and monitor their performance. Don't be afraid to make some changes in allocation on a quarterly or semiannual basis. Remember: a quick glance at a stock or ETF chart will tell you a lot in a short period of time. And don't put all of your eggs in one basket. If you own a water sector ETF, you should also consider a solar energy or biofuel component to your holdings. Maybe an index ETF is better for you, or a diversified green mutual fund is the answer.

Finally, green investments may be a part of your portfolio, but they should not be your entire portfolio. As with any other type of investment, there is no substitute for careful analysis, understanding your risk profile, paying attention to your financial needs, diversification, risk management, and always considering what your long-term goals are.

CHAPTER 14

Real Estate Investing: Getting Grounded and Rated

Real estate investing is all about location, lots, land, and rates. Traditionally, investors would say that real estate never lost its value, especially as a hedge against inflation. But as the housing crisis in 2008 showed, that is a falsehood. And although it can make for a good contributor to your investment portfolio, consider that you will have to deal with four rates—interest rates, occupancy rates, vacancy rates, and construction rates—and taxes. But, if you can handle the attack of the rates, this might be the market for you.

The Basics of the Real Estate Game

Real estate investing is a hands-on endeavor and it can be overwhelming. To be a landlord you have to learn a whole new language: closing costs, resale value, liquidity, and inspections. You also have to be ready to deal with renters and their issues, as well as needing a good attorney in case relationships with renters, prospective buyers, business partners, and contractors sour.

Because it's harder to get out of real estate investments, it's important to research the market and the business side of things before jumping in. But if you don't mind hard work and are willing to learn about this business/investment opportunity, you may find some long-term profitable investments in this sector.

And while stocks and bonds can seem conceptual in many ways, real estate is tangible. You can see land and houses and trees and rocks. And while stocks and bonds are respectively shares and loans to a company, a real estate investment is a major role reversal, which makes you the owner of the company. In other words, in real estate, you are selling shares in your company every time you rent or sell a property.

Using Leverage

Leverage is the use of borrowed money to invest. In stocks it's called margin. In real estate, it's a business loan that allows you to use someone else's money to take risk by buying a property. Leverage is a double-edged sword. When used properly it can broaden your horizons and allow you to own more property than you would with your own money. The downside is that using leverage increases your risk, and because you have to pay back the loan as you go along, it can eat into your profits. It all comes down to having the right mix of properties and leverage. If you own rental property and it's empty or you have unexpected costs such as repairs or legal problems, you could be in big trouble. The bottom line is that if you use leverage, your properties have to make enough money to at least make your monthly loan payment and cover your costs. You can make real estate investing work, but it is a business, and it will require a great deal of legwork and involvement on your part.

ALERT

Most of all, know that leverage is dangerous. Know your markets and consider whether any time is a good time to use borrowed money to start or expand your real estate business.

Your Action Plan

Here is how you can make it work. First, never borrow any more than you can afford to pay back. Read your loan contract carefully and make sure that there are no hidden clauses, especially if you want to restructure the loan to a lower interest rate in the future or to expand the time to payment. Also make sure that there is no penalty for early payment of your loan. Banks like to hide little surprises into loans, especially the loans they make to young entrepreneurs. If the loan doesn't make sense, get a CPA or advisor to look at it, or just don't take it.

While you use borrowed money, invest your own money wisely. That will improve your cash flow and broaden your opportunities. Work toward finding opportunities that will create profits in short periods of time, and give you predictable income, like flipping a house or getting tenants who pay their rent on time and reliably. If you make enough money in a short period of time, use some of it to pay your loan down or pay it off. That will leave you more money in your pocket.

The Fix and Flip Business Model

HGTV and the DIY network have glamorized the house flipping business. But don't be fooled by the TV magic. Real estate is a risky business and there are no guarantees of success. Before investing, learn as much as you can about the property and the market, and think about how things can go wrong.

An important first step is to understand the difference between an investor and a speculator. An investor is in for the long haul, while a speculator is looking to turn a quick profit and move on to the next trade. Investors are more patient and tend to look for properties that are within their means. Speculators are willing to use borrowed money and take higher risks. As a new real estate investor, it's a good idea to invest, and thus learn the ropes over time. It's also prudent to find a good advisor, an experienced investor who is willing to share her wisdom.

Novice investors in real estate who want to own physical property can get their feet wet with small rental properties, such as single- or double-family homes or even small apartment complexes with no more than four units. You can look at a fixer-upper house. Usually, the easiest properties to get started with are single-family homes due to their ease of buying and selling relative to other types of units.

FACT

Time management is a big deal in real estate. If you take a day to paint a house, you may not be saving as much money as you think. You can use that time to look for another property, especially one that is inexpensive and that you may be able to sell quickly. If you turn a $30,000 profit in 100 hours of work with the new property, you just paid yourself $300 per hour, more than enough to pay for painters.

The Fixer-Upper Dilemma

The flipper's dream is to buy an inexpensive older home for a small amount, then fix it up, and sell it for a lot more than you paid for it. And while this is plausible and can be done with frequency, it's not without risk and details. Consider the following factors when buying a fixer-upper:

- **Expertise.** In order to know your financial exposure and risk, you should know something about building design and construction in order to estimate the amount of work, money, and time that you'll have to put into the project. Figure out how much you can do yourself and how much you'll have to pay contractors or other experts to do things for you. Don't forget building material costs and to give yourself some room for the unexpected and inevitable intangibles, especially hidden plumbing and electrical surprises.
- **Patience.** Real estate is not like stock trading. Even if you are looking for short-term profits, things don't always work out the way you planned

them. Expect crazy things to happen once you start remodeling and develop patience and a sense of purpose. Also remember that even though you have turned a trash bin into a diamond, market pressures will affect your ability to sell a property. Be prepared to hang on to it for a while.

- **Inspection.** Don't buy a house without getting a professional home inspector to do a comprehensive inspection. Do your homework on this. Make sure that the inspector is thorough by checking out his references. Even the most thorough inspector won't find everything that isn't up to par, but the better ones will pick out more than the guys that are just trying to take your money.

- **Location.** Location is the most important factor in real estate. Study the neighborhood, the shopping around it, the roads, access to highways and mass transport, the schools, and recreational opportunities. Look into zoning issues and think about what kind of buyer you may want to attract. Good schools and easy shopping tend to attract young families, while easy highway access tends to attract good commercial buyers.

ESSENTIAL

In order to protect your rental property investment, you will need rental insurance and property insurance. You will need these policies aside from your homeowner's policy because your homeowner's policy won't cover any liability for alleged damages that your renters may try to blame on you or any damage done to the property by the renters.

Keep It Simple

Don't look for unconventional or niche properties. Stick to normal and conventional properties in good locations. These are the ones that will pay off over the long run. Pay special attention to any possible damages or defects in the property before you buy it. Anything that shows up after the closing will cost you money. Think about whether there will be demand for this particular type of property in five or ten years. And always keep your eyes open for special features in a property, such as a state-of-the-art kitchen or truly remarkable bathrooms or closet space.

Most importantly, gauge at what part of the market cycle you may be. If property prices have been rising astronomically for the past decade, as they did in the period leading to the 2008 crash, it may make sense to wait or to look for bargain properties. You may be able to buy premium properties on the cheap at a later time.

Common Sense Is Key

Use your common sense and your gift of observation. If you bought a house in what seemed to be a vibrant area and over the next few weeks you learn that the largest employer in the community is about to close its plant and suddenly the house next door to your property is empty, expect that your property is going to be difficult to rent, and will be difficult to sell unless you start deciding your next move quickly. It's better for you to research this kind of situation before you buy. No matter how attractive any property is, its future sale value will only be as good as its location and the local economy.

Building Wealth Through Rental Properties

When deciding about your real estate investment future, you may ask: to buy or not to buy? Yet, there is a better set of questions. What to buy? And, how to go about buying it? The answers have to do with deciding between commercial and residential property and determining which makes better sense for you at the beginning of your real estate investing process. No matter what your decision is, several things will be consistent. For example, you need to figure out how much money you will need up front, and whether that money will come from your savings or a loan. Much of what happens will depend on your financial situation and whether your bank considers you a good loan risk. The equally important point, if you're loan worthy, is what the terms of the loan will be. Perhaps the most important factor is that as a new investor it may not be wise to borrow money to invest in real estate. That's because you have to pay the loan back, and that loan payment could squeeze your cash flow. Things will get worse if you're not able to get tenants, or if you lose any tenants you may have. Remember that real estate is not like stocks and bonds. You need a lot more money to get started and to keep things rolling. It also takes time to sell a property. And during the entire time that you own the property, whether it's making money or not, you'll still have to pay the bills.

Trust Your Intuition and Do Your Homework

Beware of what you don't know. If a seller is giving you a great deal on what seems to be a premium property, something may be up. It could be anything, such as a bad economic event that is not quite known yet or something more closely related to the property, like a new freeway overpass is going to be built across the street from your potential rental place. In order to avoid being duped, always consider the following:

- Is this a prime location? When in doubt, in real estate think about the property's location; past, present, and future.
- Has this property been rented before? Try and get as much detail as possible, including the length of any rental engagement and any particular circumstances.
- How old is the property? The older the property is, the more likely that it will require a thorough inspection and a substantial repair budget.
- Is your property up to code? This is where an inspector comes in handy, as he finds out if your plumbing, electricity, foundation, and roof meet local ordinance requirements.
- How much repair work is required? Based on your inspection results you'll have an idea as to how much work the property will need. Consider what it will cost to remodel the interior for business or rental purposes. Think in as much detail as possible. Older homes may not be wired for high speed Internet and multiple phone lines for commercial purposes. And don't forget the exterior. Any landscaping, painting, and repair work will also cost you money and time.
- Are there maintenance costs? Will you need landscapers and gardeners? If you go commercial, who will pay for the janitor service? What about the alarm and other security costs?
- Are there specific zoning laws in the area? If you want to rent the property as office space, make sure that the city has designated your area as commercial. If you are thinking of owning the property as your own business, make sure that you can run that type of business in that area.

- Review the accessibility of the property. Think of what you envision the property to be. A business property needs to be well located and visible, while a summer cottage will be better if it's well hidden and private.
- Are there plans for the area in the future? If a new mall is coming, how will it affect your business property? Do you want to own a rental property across from a low-end market motel?
- Have you considered the cost of insurance? Compare costs from several agents and figure them into the overall costs of your property and its future maintenance.
- What will the effect of property taxes be on your costs? How much of a bite will they be on your profit margin or in your ability to pay back a property loan? How much of the property taxes may be a tax deduction?

If you are still game after reviewing the previous checklist, you may be cut out to be a real estate investor. If suddenly you're not all that interested, there may still be a way for you to invest through a real estate investment trust, which will be covered later in this chapter.

Choosing the Most Profitable Real Estate

If you've decided to take the plunge, you have to decide what kind of real estate makes the most sense based on your long-term goals, as it takes a long time for properties to develop and to provide a good return on your initial investment. The real question is whether you will hold a property for an extended period of time as a rental or whether you will try to flip it for a quick profit. Each method requires a distinctly different approach and will lead you to a different marketplace.

Part of the art of investing is to not only find a suitable location, but to then discern if it makes sense for what your goal is—and then you have to know what to do with it! A good place to look for properties is in an area that is being revitalized. This puts you in a place where you will have some flexibility. A good review and a thorough analysis of the current area and what's likely to happen there from a commercial and political standpoint is a must. Is this an area where people are flocking? If it is, then what is the attraction? Once you understand the dynamic, then you must consider how to tap into it in the most cost-effective and potentially profitable manner.

Considering Commercial Versus Residential Property

If your goal is to be on the commercial property side of things, look for areas where large new attractions are being built or where large companies are moving their headquarters. Think beyond just owning a building in the area and look to the possibility of setting up a business there. Consider opening a restaurant or refurbishing space that can house such a business. Try to find out what no one is doing there and try to fill that particular niche. Is there a dry cleaner in the area? Does it make sense to consider offering medical office space? Anything is possible if you take the time to study the needs of an up-and-coming area.

If you decide to go the residential property route, use the same principle but look to the different needs of your client. Families want access to shopping, good schools, restaurants, and entertainment. They also want good roads or easy access to public transportation and low crime rates. Put yourself in the renter or potential buyer's place. Would you move into this area? The key to success in both commercial and residential real estate is that you can put together the best possible package for your customer.

The Management Challenge

You've survived the buyer's stage of real estate investment. Now it's time to consider what it takes to manage your properties for maximum efficiency and income. That means brushing up on your management skills and having an eye for detail given the specific requirements of property management. Timing of maintenance and managing the cost is paramount. If you are handy you can do some of this, although it may make more sense to hire someone as you handle other things required by the property. If you hire someone to do the maintenance, you have to factor in the costs of the contractor(s) and how reliable and experienced they actually are. As a rule, contractors tend to spread their wares through multiple jobs at any one time. That can make them hard to find and hard to pin down with regard to when they will actually show up to do the job. That means that you may have to manage angry tenants during times when repairs are pending. And unlike owning stocks, you are the one that will be getting the complaint calls.

Rental Properties in Perspective

Think of it like this. Once you own rental property, you are the "land-lord." And if you're a renter, you know that means that life can get pretty interesting. Just think of being on the other side of the experience. Remember that a good landlord tends to keep her tenants, while a not-so-good one has trouble renting the house and can lose money. As a landlord, you're not protecting your own home. You are managing a source of income. That means that you have to be aware of what it takes to keep the place going. Think about the time and money that it requires and measure that against your return. Contrast the time you spend on the property to how much time you spend on your mutual funds.

Landlord-Tenant Communication

To be sure, being a good landlord is possible, and it can be profitable. An important aspect of it is in how you communicate with your tenants. Tenants should be aware of your expectations, your rules, and your regulations in advance. Don't sign a lease unless these points are addressed. Any changes should be communicated in a timely fashion in writing, and you should have proof that the tenant actually received the information.

Other Important Considerations

Also understand that it will take some time from the moment you buy the rental property to the time you will find tenants. The monthly checks won't just appear in your bank account. If you don't have the time to manage the property, hiring a professional management firm may make sense. And even though these firms take care of landscaping, maintenance, and other important issues, they charge fees. Fees can cut into your profit margin, which means that you have to calculate this into your expenses and pass these costs on to your tenants.

Real Estate Investment Trusts

If you're not quite ready to become a flipper or a landlord, you can still invest in real estate via real estate investment trusts (REITs, pronounced "reet"). A

REIT is an investment company, in many ways similar to an exchange traded mutual fund (ETF), which allows you to participate in real estate without being in the front lines. You can buy REIT shares on a stock exchange, or you can buy a mutual fund or an ETF that invests in REITs.

REITs have been around for over thirty-five years and are a convenient and fairly safe way to invest in real estate. You make money in a REIT as you do with stocks, by collecting dividends and when the share price rises. Because of the legal structure of a REIT, the business is not taxed but the shareholder is. This is what is known as a pass-through security.

What's in a REIT?

Unlike mutual funds, REITs don't buy stock in companies. Instead they buy real estate investments, usually in the form of properties or mortgages. The income, in the case of property REITs, comes from the cash generated by the property. Mortgage REITs invest in mortgages used to finance the purchase of properties. In the case of mortgage REITs, the income flows from the money generated by the mortgages. Hybrid REITs invest in a little of both. Mortgage REITs lend money to real estate investors and tend to pay a higher dividend than property REITs, but they can have a higher risk of losses because they only make money as long as the investors pay back the loans.

Why should you care about all of this? Because REITs can be attractive investments and can provide income and capital gains without the potential hassle of owning rental or commercial properties. You can get a great deal of information about REITs through the National Association of Real Estate Investment Trusts (*www.reit.com* or via their toll-free number, 1-800-3NAREIT). REITs often have their own websites, and many brokers have access to REIT information, although since REITs are an area of special expertise it makes sense to use a broker with experience in this particular area.

Comparing REITs

Picking the right REIT for your portfolio depends on multiple but very important factors. Here is a list:

- **Dividend yield.** Compare the dividend yield of the average REIT to that of the stock market. For example, in the first three months of 2014, the nineteen REITs in the S&P 500 had an average yield of 3.62%, with a range of 1.39% to 5.62%. The S&P 500 index dividend yield over the same three months was 1.96%, according to *www.reitmonitor.com*. To calculate yield, divide the dividend per share by the price of the stock. Lower stock prices will make the yield rise, and higher prices lower the yield. Generally, REITs pay better dividends than stocks.
- **Earnings growth.** To understand how much money your REIT is making, look to the funds from operations (FFO). The trend in this number tells you how well things are going. It is the net income, excluding gains or losses from property sales and debt restructuring, and including real estate depreciation.
- **What your REIT's holdings are.** Know what kinds of properties the REIT holds. It can be anything from shopping centers to office or apartment buildings, resorts, health-care facilities, or other forms of real estate such as farmland or empty land awaiting development.
- **Geographic locations.** Make sure you know where your REIT invests, nationally, regionally, or internationally.
- **Diversification.** You can buy a REIT that is diversified on its own, by buying different kinds of properties in different locations, or you can buy several different kinds of REITs. The goal is to spread the risk and potentially reduce losses.
- **Management.** The management company of your REIT is as important as the managers of a mutual fund or a company CEO and his team. The more experienced, and the better the track record of management, the more likely you are to make money over time.

ALERT

Stay in tune with the markets and interest rates. REITs are as interest-rate sensitive as real estate. During periods of falling real estate prices and higher interest rates, REITs tend to fall in price and can produce losses even if dividend yields rise. True dividends may actually fall during these periods, as the REIT may find it difficult to make money due to a bad real estate market.

Remember to always do your homework. A REIT is like any other investment. Check it out, and know as much as possible about it before investing.

REIT Mutual Funds and ETFs

You can also own REITs through traditional mutual funds and exchange traded mutual funds (ETFs). Morningstar (*www.morningstar.com*) has great data on REIT funds, and most of the major mutual fund companies offer mutual funds dedicated to REITs. Many of them are no-load funds and most pay quarterly dividends, which makes them attractive as income-producing vehicles. NAREIT also has great data on funds and offers a list on their website at *www.reit.com/investing*. There you will find great tools, such as up-to-date news on the industry, a directory of REITs with phone numbers and websites, a list of REIT ETFs, a portfolio optimizer tool, which lets you test the risk/reward profile of a mix of REITs for your portfolio, as well as a REIT portfolio app.

Tracking Your REITs

You can find the price of your REIT in newspapers, through your broker, and through any financial website that offers online quotes. REITs have symbols like stocks, so you just type the number in the quote box and you'll see how it's doing. REIT mutual funds and ETFs are like other similar securities, and you can keep up with their price online as well.

All in all, real estate investment is not for everyone, but it can be a profitable endeavor. REITs can offer a simpler, less time-consuming, and less labor-intensive way to participate in this investment area.

CHAPTER 15

Taking More Risks

Risky investments are not for everyone because they are about the possibility of making big gains and suffering equally big losses. And while most investors are more than happy to make big bucks, especially over short periods of time, no one enjoys watching their money evaporate. This chapter is all about the ins and outs, the good and the bad, of risky investments and risky investment techniques and how they may or may not be something that makes sense for your portfolio.

Risky Strategies: The Double-Edged Sword

Risk refers to the balance between winning and losing. In investing, it's all about how risk affects the value of your portfolio. And while most investors are willing to avoid risk, some are more than happy to embrace it, along with the potential for losing large amounts of money. The reason for this type of risk-taking behavior is that sometimes you can make a lot of money in a hurry by taking big chances. That's because risky strategies involve leverage, which is investing with borrowed money. The more leverage, the more chance of big gains but also of potentially catastrophic losses, which is why risk is a double-edged sword.

There are two ways to take risks. One is by using alternative or derivative securities, such as options, and the other is by using risky techniques. Often, the two are combined, and the risk/reward ratio can reach levels of significant unpredictability. Alternative securities can be an acquired taste, but can include securities such as initial public offerings (IPOs), commodities, options, futures, and leveraged ETFs. Alternative investment strategies include the use of margin, short selling, and hedging. By combining alternative securities and alternative techniques, you can give your portfolio a big pop to the upside in a hurry. But you can also lose big bucks in the blink of an eye. Losses when you use these techniques without truly understanding them can be as much as your whole investment, and in some cases even more than your original stake. The bottom line is that investing should not be like a trip to Vegas, which is why this chapter is all about developing an understanding of these types of investments and how to use them.

Selling Short and Using Margin

Short selling is the opposite of going long. "Going long" is Wall Street jargon for buying stocks, bonds, or other assets. Long investors are hoping that their assets rise in price. "Going short" or short selling is the opposite. Investors who short assets are hoping that prices drop.

Selling Short

Short sellers borrow stock, usually from their broker's own stock, and sell it. If the stock drops in price, the short seller buys it back at the lower price. His profit is the difference in the price at which he borrowed it, hopefully higher, and the price at which he bought it back, hopefully lower. It makes little sense, but that's how Wall Street is sometimes, downright tricky, which is why short selling is not for new investors.

Here is an example of how it might work. Jane has been watching Google and thinks that it's about to start a meaningful decline due to a bad earnings report. So Jane borrows 100 shares of Google at $500. Jane just put up $50,000 and owes her broker 100 shares of Google. Google does indeed have a bad earnings report and shares drop $20. Jane buys $100 shares for $480 and pockets $2,000. If Google's price didn't move up or down, Jane might have gotten cold feet and gotten out close to even. But if Google had beaten its earnings expectations and the stock would have rallied, say $20 to $520, Jane would have lost $2,000 plus the purchase price of the stock, totaling $52,000. If Jane got stubborn, hoping that Google would eventually fall, but the stock kept gaining, Jane's losses could be even worse.

Here is something else to remember: Jane has to pay commission on any trade, so those costs are also included, whether the trade goes her way or not. Also, if Google had paid a dividend during the time that Jane was short, Jane would have passed that dividend to the broker.

Margin Buying

Margin buying is related to short selling in two ways. One is that it involves borrowing money. The other is that in order to sell stocks short, you need a margin account. When you use margin to buy stocks, you use some of your own money, and some of your broker's money. Usually, this is about a 50-50 split. Thus, margin buying lets you buy more stock with less of your own money. The shares you buy count as collateral for your loan.

And while this may sound like a good deal, it's another side of the double-edged sword, because margin is a form of leverage. If your stock goes up, you're okay. If the price drops, you've got some problems because your margin account needs to have at least 25% of the value of the stock you borrowed by federal law. Your broker may have a higher margin requirement as well, which is why you should read your margin agreement carefully before signing it. When your balance drops below the maintenance margin set by your broker, you will get a "margin call," which is Wall Street lingo for "you need to put up more money." You can do that by writing a check or by selling the stock at a loss and hoping that it covers your debt.

Experienced traders with short-term strategies, such as hedge funds, who use sophisticated and often technical analysis–based techniques, often use margin. Even these traders can get into trouble, though, as short-term volatility and big drops in the stock market are often attributed to hedge fund bets that went wrong and triggered margin calls.

Here is an example. Jane, that crazy risk taker, wants to buy $10,000 worth of Apple, but only wants to put up $5,000 of her own money. Apple shares fall in price by $2,000. That means that the current share price is $7,000 less than the $5,000 loan in her margin transaction and is $500 less than her maintenance margin. Jane's choice is to put up another $500 or sell her shares at a loss and pay off the loan.

Initial Public Offerings

Another risky strategy is that of buying initial public offerings, or IPOs. An IPO is what happens on the day when a company first goes public and the stock makes its debut on the stock exchange. On that first day, the gains on the price can be extreme, and so can the losses. By selling stock to the public through an IPO, a company raises money without taking on debt. It's also an opportunity, in many cases, for early investors to cash in some of their shares and be rewarded for their initial risk. New investors, impressed with the company's performance, buy into the company at this stage in hopes of participating in the company's good fortunes.

Investment banks, such as Goldman Sachs, are the underwriters of the IPO. That means that they are the ones that handle the details of bringing the company's shares to market and collect fees for doing the work. The major stumbling block for an IPO, if there is one, is whether the SEC allows it to happen, based on whether the process has met the criteria established in the Securities Act of 1933. Because investment banks are thorough and because their reputation often depends on the success of an IPO, it's very rare for this process to go awry.

Should You Get In on IPOs?

The lure of making big bucks in a short period of time is significant. But the downside to IPOs is also worth considering. For one thing, small investors don't have much of a chance to get shares at the initial offering price, which is often significantly lower than where the shares can trade in a few minutes' time. That's because professional investors, who buy large blocks of stock, tend to swoop up the initial supply at the lower prices and then "flip" them in a few minutes to pocket the quick profit produced when the stock pops. As a small investor, even if you have an experienced broker handling your IPO transactions, you don't have much of a chance against the deep-pocket professional. Thus, although it may sound attractive, it makes sense to add IPO stocks to your watch list and see how things go with them for a while before you take the plunge.

FACT

Companies sometimes sell stock after their initial public offering. This process is called a secondary offering, and it's done to raise money for some purpose, such as buying back debt or financing an acquisition. Secondary offerings sometimes will issue a special class of nonvoting stock and are usually not as big a news item as is an IPO.

Facebook's IPO: When Things Go Wrong

A perfect example of an IPO debacle was what happened with Facebook, whose shares plunged after the IPO due to technical problems at Nasdaq and what some in the financial press reported as self-inflicted problems by the company in the way it handled some of the crucial financial disclosures in its prospectus. The bottom line is that the stock, which was hyped by its underwriters, including Morgan Stanley, to a very high level, flopped in its debut, and according to multiple sources, small investors got saddled with the short-term losses that followed in the next few weeks. That's because the smart-money large investors who went to Facebook's road show presentations were made aware of the vague statements in the prospectus, and they avoided the stock. The flip side, and the side that supports being patient, is that the stock rallied nicely within a few weeks of its IPO. Small investors who had been patient were able to pick up shares at a much lower price.

Commodities and Precious Metals

Commodities are the raw materials that are used to manufacture products ranging from food to high-tech gadgets. The major factor influencing commodity prices is supply, or the ease of availability of the product. Even the fear of a decrease in supply, such as when the Iraq wars erupted in the Middle East, can send commodity prices higher. The trick, when investing in commodities, is to have a good handle on the supply, and then be aware of when there might be a spike in demand. Commodities, even when owned indirectly through a mutual fund or ETF, are an important component of a diversified portfolio.

Commodities

Investing in commodities requires a fair amount of homework but can be profitable since, unlike stocks, there is a certain everyday connection to them. Aside from investing directly in commodities, keeping up with the price activity in this area of the markets may provide useful information about other commodities as well as the industrial and market sectors where any individual commodity plays a vital role. Here are some examples of everyday commodities that may be worth considering for investment:

- **Lumber** is used in homebuilding and furniture. Generally speaking, a housing boom is bullish for lumber prices.
- **Oil** is a centerpiece of the global economy. Aside from being a commodity in and of itself, it is also an influence on gasoline, heating oil, and natural gas prices. Oil is a major contributor to the price of chemicals. Thus, any factor that affects oil can and often does have a significant influence on other commodities and industrial sectors.

- **Cotton** remains a major global player, as it is used in clothing and other lesser-known products such as coffee filters.
- **Wheat** is a key commodity given its central role in food around the world.
- **Corn** is the most widely traded grain in the world, with uses in food, animal feed, biofuels, and building materials.
- **Gold, silver, and platinum** are perhaps the most popular commodities given their use in jewelry. Silver is an important industrial metal, while platinum is central to the automobile industry given its use as a major engine component in catalytic converters.
- **Coffee, cocoa, and sugar** are known collectively as "the softs." Anyone who needs his morning cup of java or enjoys a candy bar can appreciate these three commodities.

The best way for nonprofessional investors, at any stage of experience but especially in the early stage of investing, to participate in these markets is through a mutual fund or an ETF. An ETF may be superior because of the ease of trading throughout the day. This is particularly important when commodity prices are going through a volatile period.

ESSENTIAL

If you are interested in commodity ETFs, the Deutsche Bank Power-Shares Commodity DB Index Tracking ETF (NYSE: DBC) is a broad index of commodities and offers diversification. Holdings include oil, gold, as well as a batch of agricultural commodities. It's a good idea to track this ETF's price and general behavior for a few months or longer before considering investing in it, as it can be volatile.

Gold

Gold is a different type of animal. While it may make sense to invest in other commodities via paper through mutual funds or ETFs, gold gives you a more practical set of choices. You can choose to invest in gold indirectly through paper assets, but you can actually own physical gold, via jewelry, gold bars, or bullion coins, fairly easily.

Gold bullion is the pure, raw form of gold before it is shaped into bars. This may be the most difficult way to own gold as an individual investor. Gold bars must be made of at least 99.5% gold bullion and weigh a uniform 400 troy ounces (the standard weight measure of gold). Gold bullion coins are legal tender, although they are not used as currency very often anymore. Their worth is usually more than their face value, although that depends on their weight and the market price of gold at any one time. Gold coins tend to be popular investments, especially among collectors.

Trading Currencies

For new investors it can be difficult to see how you can make money by trading money. But currencies, although not the best market for a newbie, can still be lucrative. The simplest currency trade is what anyone does when they visit a foreign exchange booth while traveling abroad. In fact, currency trading, known as FX for foreign exchange, is a huge market, with over $2 trillion exchanging hands on a daily basis.

Most of the trading involves the major global currencies:

1. The U.S. Dollar (also known as the Greenback)
2. The Pound Sterling (U.K.)
3. The Japanese Yen
4. The Euro
5. The Canadian Dollar (a.k.a. the Loonie and the Canuck Buck)
6. The Swiss Franc (sometimes called the Swissie)
7. The Australian Dollar (also called the Aussie)
8. The New Zealand Dollar (referred to as the Kiwi)

Currencies trade in pairs. For example the USD/Yen pairing refers to the exchange rate between the U.S. dollar and the Japanese yen. The value of this pairing will be different from other pairings, such as the Euro/Yen, because currency pairings are only based on the relative value of one currency versus another.

FACT

Currency traders are known to be eccentric. And their terminology bears this out. For example, the unit of price movement in a currency is called a "pip." Thus, a three-pip move in a currency means that it has moved three basic trading units. In comparison, when a stock or a bond changes in price, it is considered a "tick." Another unique nickname is the one given to the pairing between the U.S. dollar and the U.K. pound sterling. This pairing is referred to as "the cable." So if you read an article about the price change in "the cable," you'll know it's in reference to the U.S. dollar and the pound sterling.

The Unique World of Currency Trading

Currency traders have their own language, and the currency markets are significantly different than the stock, bond, and commodity markets, where there is usually an exchange, a regulatory agency, and a set of verifiable rules. Currencies trade "over the counter." That means that every trade is between two private parties through a trading platform provided by a dealer, usually a bank, that operates only as a middle man, in the sense of providing quotes and housing the account.

And although that may sound frightening, the currency markets work because they are self-regulating. Because large corporations and big trading houses participate in them, they have a vested interest in self-policing. Just to be clear, though, this is not a market for inexperienced investors. If you must consider it, make sure that your currency dealer is registered with the National Futures Association, and they are likely to participate in binding arbitration should you have a problem. Also, don't open a foreign currency trading account without reading the agreement first.

FACT

Currency trading may be useful to you if you are a night owl since it goes on twenty-four hours per day, starting at 5:00 P.M. on Sunday and going on continuously all week until 4:00 P.M. on Friday.

Think Interest Rates When Trading Currencies

Aside from the lack of an exchange, the nuts and bolts of currency trading is a bit different than with stocks, bonds, and mutual funds. When you buy and sell currencies, there is an interest rate component. Currency buyers earn interest, while sellers pay interest.

It sounds a bit on the goofy side, but it does work. First you sell a currency. Then you use the proceeds to buy another. In reality, the transactions occur simultaneously. If you are the seller, you pay interest to the buyer. If you are the buyer, you get interest along with owning the currency.

Each currency has a particular interest rate associated with it, which is calculated in increments of $\frac{1}{100}$ of a percent, also known as a basis point. This works out as follows: If you sold a currency with a rate of 500 points and bought a currency with a rate of 700 points, your net return is 200 basis points (2%).

ALERT

Currency trading is not for the uninitiated. Most online currency trading platforms let you do paper trading without using real money. It's a good idea to use this technology in order to work out the kinks of your strategy before you actually plunge into this kind of trading.

Deciphering Derivatives

Derivatives are investments that derive their value from another investment. Without the underlying asset—as the related investment is called—a derivative is worthless. What that boils down to is that a derivative is a bet on the price of a related investment and that derivative trading is akin to gambling more on the direction of the price of the underlying asset than on the real value of it.

All derivatives are contractual agreements between two parties. Commonly used derivatives are options, futures, swaps, and forward contracts. Derivatives can be written on stocks, stock indexes, bonds, currencies, and commodities, as well as weather data, the size of crops, or even more esoteric things, such as the derivatives that nearly crashed the world economy in 2008. Those derivatives were written as bets on whether people would actually make their mortgage payments.

The Facts on Options

The most commonly traded derivatives are options based on stocks. An option gives the holder the right, but not the obligation, to buy or sell the underlying security at a specific price by a specific date. In other words, the option trader is betting that the price of a security will move as she expects and as much as she expects. The key to options trading is to make a bet on the direction of the move and the magnitude before the option expires. Stock options are the most common of options, which is why this section will focus on them the most.

The largest options exchange in the United States is the Chicago Board Options Exchange (*www.cboe.com*). The website has a huge wealth of information, including options symbols and other data that can be helpful in analyzing the stock and bond market.

Stock Options

Options trading has a language all of its own. Here are some basic facts and terms:

- **Call option.** This option lets you buy 100 shares of XYZ stock at the specified price.
- **Put option.** Put options let you sell 100 shares of XYZ stock at the specified price.
- **Expiration date.** This is the date on which the option becomes worthless.
- **Strike price.** This is the specified price of the stock on which the option is based.
- Option buyers are **buyers**. Option sellers are known as **writers**. When you write an option, you give buyers the opportunity to buy or sell the underlying security at the underlying price.

For example: If you bought a May 2014 55 Call option on XYZ stock, you would have the option of buying 100 shares of XYZ stock on the expiration date of the option, May of 2014. If you buy the 55 Call option when the stock is at $35 and it rises to $55, you could exercise the option and buy a stock that is selling at $55 for only $35. You could then turn around and sell it for $55, pocketing the nice profit. If the stock falls below the strike price, you would let the option expire worthless. A call option has unlimited upside potential, while your risk is only what you paid for the option if it expires worthless. A put option can be a risky proposition if the stock rises in price.

The value of an option is influenced by four different factors: the underlying price of the stock, the strike price, the cost of holding a position in the underlying stock, and an estimate of the future volatility of the stock.

LEAPS

LEAPS (Long Term Equities Participation Securities) are long-term options. If you wanted to bet on the direction of a stock over the next several years, you would buy LEAPS, which don't usually expire for two to three years and sometimes last for five to ten years. Beyond that distinction, LEAPS are similar to regular options, except that they are fewer in number, although you can find LEAPS for the most heavily traded stocks.

Employee Stock Options

Employee stock options became buzz worthy in the 1990s when the dot-com boom made them very popular. You may be aware of them, and you may even have gotten some or may get some in the future. These are different than the listed options that trade in the markets. Unlike the listed options, there is no third party. Instead, employee stock options are a direct contract between the employer and the employee. Here are a few important facts about them:

- Employers use them as incentives to encourage hard work from employees.
- There may be some tax advantages associated with these options.

- They have different time frames compared to listed options. Employee options have more time constraints associated with them. Mandatory holding periods before exercise can be as long as one to ten years.

Employee options are often used by startup companies or companies that are in the midst of rapid periods of growth. Often these companies have plans for going public at some point in the future and use these options to both entice, recruit, and retain good workers in order to keep the growth momentum moving forward. They really gained a great deal of fame in the early years of the dot-com boom. The downside is that if the company goes bust or underperforms, it could be difficult to cash these options in.

Trading Futures

A futures contract, unlike an options contract, is an obligation to buy or sell an asset at the expiration of the contract. The reason for this is that futures were designed for farmers in expectation of delivery of their crops. Most futures contracts are based on commodities, such as wheat, corn, oil, or cattle. But the markets have expanded beyond commodities to include stock indexes, bonds, metals, and currencies. Even more interesting are the futures contracts that deal with housing prices and weather.

Trading futures is a risky business. Prices move rapidly and tend to be volatile. Because of the pricing structure of the contracts, one tick (basic unit of price in any contract) can mean that you gain or lose a fair amount of money in a very short period of time.

Here is an example. A West Texas Intermediate crude oil futures contract contains 1,000 barrels of crude oil. The minimum tick is 0.01 or one cent. Each tick is worth $10 per contract. If the price of crude oil moves up $1 (100 ticks), you just made $1,000 per contract. If the price moves the other way, you could lose $1,000 per contract. If you are a big trader and you are holding 100 contracts, a $1 move is worth $100,000.

In conclusion, alternative investments, especially derivatives, are not for the novice investor. Over time, as you gain experience, you may slowly move into these areas. Most professionals, though, will tell you that these types of investments are for trading, not for long-term buy and hold strategies.

CHAPTER 16

Working with a Financial Advisor

If you're wondering why a book about self-directed investing has a chapter on financial advisors, consider that every child needs a bit of parenting. If you are a serious investor, and you apply yourself, you will likely succeed over time. But in the early stages, an advisor can be a mentor. Even if an advisor does not make your investment decisions and is not holding your hand, an experienced second opinion can come in handy. This chapter is about finding out what kind of advisor makes sense for you and how you may make the best use of such a potentially useful tool.

What Kind of Advice Do You Need?

If you are an independent person you may wonder if an advisor is a good idea. But think about it: You are about to put real money on the line. Even if you are naturally cut out to be an investor, having a little help in the early stages may be a good idea. Much depends on how much sense the concepts involved in market analysis and asset allocation make to you. If you are comfortable with these aspects of investing, you probably don't need an advisor. Yet, if you can't decide whether you want to own growth stocks or whether bonds make sense, you are more likely to need an advisor.

The Personal Survey

A good way to mull over the decision to get a financial advisor or not is by asking some important questions and conducting a personal financial survey. Consider the following: Does the thought of managing your own portfolio make you uncomfortable? Are you always second-guessing your decisions? Would you be able to buy stocks in a down market or when there is short- or longer-term decline in the markets? Are you willing to put in the time to analyze market trends, to look for the best-performing sectors, and to crunch numbers and evaluate individual securities, such as mutual funds, stocks, or exchange traded mutual funds? Perhaps the most important question: How strong is your resilience after a failure? Is your favorite TV channel CNBC? Is your first morning read the *Wall Street Journal* or *Investor's Business Daily*? If you answered yes to many of these questions, it's likely that you are cut out to be a self-directed individual investor. If you are a real nut about investing, you may even want to consider a career as an investment advisor. There is a good market for this type of professional these days, especially an able one.

ESSENTIAL

A good financial advisor should be a true consultant, working with you on developing a long-term investment plan and asset allocation strategies to help you achieve your goals. Your advisor may also help you with budgeting, tax, and estate planning and guide you in setting up college savings plans. Without an advisor, you have to do all these things on your own.

If, however, you find that doing your homework and agonizing over which mutual fund to own, you hate reading the financial press, or you just don't have the time, you may be someone who needs to consider hiring a professional.

The Time Trade

A significant factor when deciding on whether you will use a financial advisor is time. It takes a long time to be a serious investor. Thus, a financial advisor may be a choice based on the time constraints of your life, and what you are getting in return for more time with your family or work is investment expertise.

Another time-related issue is that at the beginning, you will, and you should, take longer to make even the simplest of decisions. Having someone who can assist you in speeding things up while providing sound advice makes sense. Finally, if you eventually want to make your own decisions, you can only use an advisor for the first few months or the first year in order to expand your own knowledge base. Your advisor may be an excellent source of learning materials, such as books or websites that you can begin to use to gain insight and experience before slowly weaning yourself away and doing your own portfolio management.

What Can You Expect from a Financial Advisor?

The simple answer to the question is that different kinds of advisors provide different kinds of services. The key is to first be as knowledgeable as possible, and then to choose the right type of advisor to complement your own knowledge, risk profile, and personality. Your goal should be to find an advisor that helps you gain confidence and insight and that helps you to make sound financial decisions.

In order to find the right one for you, here are some of the choices:

- A money manager is someone to whom you delegate the decisions after a thorough consultation about the style and purpose of your investing. Some money managers will only do a certain kind of investing, such as aggressive or income-related securities. Once you choose your money manager, you will leave all the decisions to him and check his progress on statements or when you have conferences.

- Financial planners help you map out your long-term strategies and offer investment advice. The difference between planners and money managers is that you make the final call about pulling the trigger.
- Analysts and advisors focus on giving you information but are not involved in planning.

Financial professionals, regardless of the type you choose, will send you at least quarterly reports with details about the status of your accounts. It's a good idea to meet with them more often than quarterly if possible and to discuss the results in person. This helps you both develop your relationship and may also give you an opportunity to learn a few things. You can be as active as you want to or can be, but it's a good idea to keep close tabs on what's going on. Remember: your financial professional has other clients, and it's not always easy to keep up with everything. What this means is that you should work with a good professional that is available and willing to spend time discussing your account with you. If you can't get face time with your advisor or she never returns your calls on time, find another. Look at it this way: Even if you have a small account, you are still paying a fee for her services. That means that you should have a reasonable amount of personal access.

The Advisor's Roles

Your advisor should monitor your portfolio, and review and discuss any changes in allocation or investment choices that might make sense. Your advisor should also monitor the markets and let you know of any potential concerns or significant events that will affect your account's balance and performance. Most of all, your advisor should keep you from becoming emotional if the markets turn volatile. Her job is to keep you focused on your long-term goals and provide the tools to get you there.

Where a good advisor comes in handy is in a down market. During these periods, the advisor's job is to keep you from losing big amounts of money and to preserve your wealth. The best advisors are the ones that minimize your losses and manage your emotions. A good portfolio manager, whether she manages a billion-dollar mutual fund or your modest account, should have a sense of timing about her and should be able to make changes in your asset allocation if needed. This might be a simple thing, such as not investing your newly deposited cash as she waits for a better opportunity, or advising you that maybe you should take some profits after a mutual fund has had a good run for the past few months. More importantly, the advisor should be able to communicate these strategies and changes to you and make sure that you are comfortable with what she did and why.

Shopping for the Right Financial Advisor

Once you decide that you would like to use the services of an advisor, it's equally important to find the one that makes sense for you. An easy trap is to hire one with a long-term track record without considering other aspects of the job. Consider whether this person who will be managing your money in one form or another is someone that you can get along with. Look at his firm or whether he is self-employed. Get details about the services provided. Look at samples of monthly or quarterly statements and make sure that you will understand what they say. If he works for a big company, make sure that they aren't or haven't been under investigation for fraudulent practices. Check into their customer service. Ask detailed questions about how well insured the company is against fraud and whether the advisor goes to periodic continuing education courses. Most of all, ask him about his successes and failures and what he tends to do in down markets. Ask to see some results if possible.

ALERT

Beware the commission advisor. Before you sign any agreement or pay for any services from a financial advisor, find out how she gets paid for taking care of your account. Sometimes advisors are paid bonuses and extra fees for selling you specific high-fee products that may or may not fit your needs. These advisors may also tack on management fees while the only thing they've actually done for you is to sell you high load mutual funds in order to pad their commission earnings.

There is what seems to be an alphabet soup in the certifications of financial professionals. Think of it this way: You wouldn't want a radiology technician (RRT) to take out your appendix. This is the job of a medical doctor (MD) trained as a surgeon. The same thing applies to your money. You want the right person for the right job. If you want a high-level, aggressive stock trader for your advisor, you may not be well served by the same fellow who handles your car insurance. So while this letter jumble can be confusing, there is little you can do about it other than to make sense of it by doing some research on what each of these certifications mean before you make a decision about whether this is the advisor you want to do business with.

Certified Financial Planner (CFP)

An advisor who has earned the CFP certification has put in her time and has experience in virtually every area of financial planning, from the study of the stock market and individual stocks to the intricacies of estate planning. A CFP gains certification through a rigorous program that involves a standardized curriculum, requires passing a certification examination, requires work experience that meets certification requirements, and requires passing the CFP board's fitness standards for conduct, a stringent set of ethics guidelines. The criteria and the requirements for certification are created, monitored, and enforced by the Certified Financial Planner Board of Standards (*www.cfp.net*). CFPs specialize in creating long-term financial plans and providing the strategies required to meet goals.

Chartered Life Underwriter (CLU)

These are insurance professionals, certified by The American College, that pass through rigorous training and licensure programs aimed at the insurance field. They have to pass eight courses, meet minimum experience standards, and follow a strict code of ethics in order to become licensed. They are also required to undergo high-level continuing education.

A CLU's expertise goes beyond your life insurance and includes training in estate and retirement planning. But while a CLU may make sense for your longer-term strategies, another financial professional may better serve you when it comes to stocks, bonds, mutual funds, and real estate investment trusts.

Chartered Financial Consultant (ChFC)

These professionals are also accredited by The American College and are often CLUs, but with added extras. In order to earn the extra letters, they delve into every area of financial planning from the client's perspective. Their goal is to customize a plan based on your financial know-how, position, and goals, to put the plan in motion, and to keep it on track. After they complete the program, they must pass the requisite exams and must demonstrate three years of experience in the industry before they can call themselves ChFCs. These professionals can become a one-stop shop for you, as they are well versed in tax planning, investments, insurance, retirement, and estate planning.

Personal Financial Specialist (PFS)

A certified public accountant (CPA) with additional financial planning qualifications is known as a personal financial specialist. This type of professional may be worth looking for, given their intricate and intimate knowledge of the tax code. This particular aspect of financial planning could be useful when you are looking to minimize the tax burden of your investment portfolio.

FACT

CPAs must complete additional educational requirements as demanded by the American Institute of Certified Public Accountants (AICPQ) in order to become a PFS. Another way to achieve this certification is to previously have CFP or ChFC designation and accreditation.

Keeping both the CPA and PFS designations requires continuing education and adherence to strict ethical guidelines. A PFS can be very helpful in determining your net worth and your retirement needs, and can help you formulate the right strategies for your long-term goals. The tax planning expertise is also an added bonus.

Registered Investment Advisor (RIA)

This is the certification that most advisors who are primarily money managers receive. To become an RIA, you have to pass a state certification test. Some RIAs are also brokers. Others are certified financial planners or CPAs. The reason for becoming an RIA is solely to manage active client accounts. Basically, anyone who passes the test, follows the continuing education and ethical directives of their state, and runs a clean shop can become an RIA. The state securities board or the Securities and Exchange Commission regulates RIAs. The Securities and Exchange Commission usually regulates those who manage more than $25 million in accounts, although there are several exemptions both to who must register as an advisor and who must regulate them.

How Much Will It Cost?

Much of your cost depends on what type of advisor you choose. As a general rule, though, financial advice is not cheap. At the same time, advisors are required to give you their costs up front along with a detailed list of what your money will be buying. There isn't one single payment arrangement for advisors. That's why you need to get the facts up front from each advisor that you consider before you make your decision. At the end of your interview process, you should have a good idea as to what you are paying for and whether it is worth it.

ESSENTIAL

You may be put off by advisor fees. And you may have good reason to not hire someone, especially if they are expensive and not all that good. However, it may make sense, if you know that the advisor is good, to consider negotiating with them about their fees or discussing a different fee structure than what they normally offer.

The three most common fee structures are commissions, flat fees, and fees based on a percentage of your assets under management. There may also be some transaction fees, below minimum balance fees, and account maintenance fees. Some advisors, especially money managers, charge a combination of fees, such as a flat fee for office and materials expenses and a separate fee based on a percentage of assets under management. The one constant expense, in addition to the advisory fee, that you will incur will be brokerage fees.

Commissions

Advisors who get paid via commissions make money by selling you something, like a mutual fund or an annuity in the case of a banker or an insurance agent, or in the case of stockbrokers by trading your account. Much of the time, commission-based advisors are ethical and scrupulous. Unfortunately some are not and they prey on novice investors. For that reason, it may make better sense for you to use a fee-based advisor.

Flat Fees

Fee-only advisors get paid an annual fee. You are their source of income and their fee is not based on your assets or how well your account does. Sometimes, these advisors get fees from mutual fund companies and brokerage houses for having certain kinds of securities in your portfolio. They need to tell you that they do this. If they don't and you find out later, you should fire them. Period.

Percent of Assets

This is the way that money managers get paid. A money manager, or a registered investment advisor, usually charges 1% to 3% of your total assets under management annually to manage your account. You usually pay the fee on a quarterly basis (0.25% to 0.75%) whether the advisor makes money or loses money for you during the quarter. Smaller accounts are sometimes charged larger fees, which fall if the account grows. Money managers tend to focus on larger accounts and are often active traders. As with anything else in investing, getting all the information you can up front will help you make a better decision.

What's Best for You?

More than anything else, you need to be realistic. If you have a small account but you need advice, a consulting arrangement may make sense. You can use a financial planner to help you put together a plan and consider a quarterly or biannual conference with her, or just make contact when you have a question. For estate planning, a CLU may make sense. If you come into a large sum of money from an inheritance, bonus, or a promotion, you may want to talk to a registered investment advisor and retain a good PFS. Above all things, make sure you know what you are paying for, keep up with your portfolio, participate in the decision making process, ask questions if something doesn't seem right, and don't hesitate to move your money if you're not getting the service that you're being charged for.

How to Find an Advisor

Finding an advisor might seem similar to finding your soulmate. It makes sense to take your time and to get it right early in the game. Try to get a good referral from someone you trust, a friend or a family member. You may not keep that particular advisor, but at least you'll get started with someone with a track record and a good reputation. If that doesn't deliver the goods, you can get good recommendations from the National Association of Personal Financial Advisors, the American Institute of Certified Public Accountants, the Society of Financial Service Professionals, and the International Association of Registered Financial Consultants. Take your time. You don't want to get this wrong.

CHAPTER 17

Doing It Yourself

Investing is a personal thing—there are no two people who put their money to work in the markets in the same way. At the same time, deciding to manage your own money is a big decision. Yet, if you are an independent, thoughtful, patient, and adventurous person, this—the golden age of DIY investing—could be your perfect time. Because of online trading and the wealth of information that is available on the Internet, there is almost no reason why you can't be your own money manager. This chapter is all about helping you make the decision to do it yourself and setting you on the right path.

How Much Work Are You Willing to Do?

To manage or not to manage your own money: That is the proverbial, if not altogether Shakespearean, question. Maybe more to the point is asking yourself how hard you are willing to work to grow your nest egg. Sure, anyone can pick stocks and mutual funds. But, it's not that easy. Much of the work involved in managing money involves study and analysis. The development of a routine that starts with your morning coffee and a review of the action in the overnight markets and keeps up with what lies ahead is not appealing to many people. But if you are managing your own portfolio, you are a money manager. And money managers spend a lot of time worrying about their portfolio and making sure that things are headed in the right direction. To be sure, this kind of routine is something that doesn't develop overnight. But it is something that you may want to work toward if you are serious about managing your own portfolio.

In the Beginning

It makes sense to consider a stepwise approach to manage a slow and steady progression from depending on someone to manage your portfolio to managing it yourself. Here are some things that you can do immediately that will help you manage your time and get you to being your own money manager faster. Consider that good financial planning involves more than your investments. Other components include insurance, estate planning, and tax preparation and management. So take inventory of your needs and divide the labor as follows.

- **Formulate the plan.** You can consult a good financial planner to help you put together, monitor, and adjust your long-term financial plan.
- **Get a grip on your taxes.** If you have a good CPA, there is no reason for you to become a tax expert. That doesn't mean that you shouldn't remain involved in your tax preparation and know the impact of investments on your taxes. But a CPA will always know more than you about taxes. Meet with her regularly and make sure that you are both on the same page.
- **Protect your life, your home, and your future.** Life insurance is cheap when you're young and may be the best investment anyone can make,

especially when you have a family. The same can be said for estate planning, which you may want to work on in the future.

- **Stay connected.** Keep up with the big picture regarding your financial situation, but let your team of experts handle the details of the other important components of your financial plan. By forming a team of experts to handle the other important aspects of your financial plan, you leave yourself time to manage your portfolio.

Online Investing

The greatest advance in the history of the financial markets for the individual investor was the widespread growth and the rapid improvement of the online world. Because of this phenomenon, you have access to a world of real-time information and the ability to manage your investments yourself with instant feedback. Learn to use it and make it your money management home.

FACT

You're only as good as your "trading rig" (jargon for your computer setup used in online investing). If you're still using Windows XP as your operating system, you need to upgrade. Also, don't scrimp on security and on good programs that keep your computer clean of malware and viruses. Your financial accounts can and will be hacked if you don't protect your computer. You can find excellent reviews and links to trial versions of great computer security programs at *www.cnet.com*.

The Ups and the Downs of Online Investing

The biggest advantages of online investing for DIY investors are: control of their accounts, vast access to excellent and timely information, and the ability to make decisions and change asset allocation or strategies rapidly. When you add the convenience of 24-7 access to your financial information, the efficiency of having your data in front of you instantly, and the low prices of commissions for online accounts, you have a great tool at your disposal. The downside is that you are on your own when it comes to making decisions about what to invest in and how to go about it. The good thing is that because of the way online investing is set up, you can learn to manage the potential negative aspects of the dynamic by being disciplined, thinking things through, and preparing yourself for a very rewarding experience if you take the time to get it right.

As you become more sophisticated, you may want to get into pro-style chart analysis. Make sure that your home computer and your smartphone can handle the big data associated with stock charts. Slow downloads can kill a good buying or selling opportunity. The bottom line is that, as with anything else, online investing requires a thorough understanding of what you're doing and its potential pitfalls. Here are some practices that will keep you from being sorry that you became a DIY online investor:

- **Are you well connected?** Internet access is a basic necessity if you are to develop an online investing presence. If you don't have a good connection at home, at work, or through your smartphone, you could be in trouble. Most experienced home-based traders and investors have at least two Internet connections; one that they use routinely and another for when the first one fails. Maybe you should consider cable and DSL with home Wi-Fi, along with choosing a broker that has a good smartphone app for account access. To be sure, having all these backup systems could get expensive. So maybe you can start with DSL or cable along with a good smartphone setup and expand your access options in the future as your account grows and you can afford more. Just be aware of the fact that if you are not well connected and a negative event in the markets happens, you may find yourself in the uncomfortable position of not knowing what your accounts are doing.
- **Setting up your online account.** Make sure that you choose the right type of online trading account. With some online brokers, you will set up a mutual fund account that only allows you to make exchanges between their own funds. If that's all you want to do, that's fine. If you want to trade stocks, ETFs, or mutual funds from different fund families, you will need a brokerage account. If you are interested in short selling and trading options, you will need a margin account. As a novice investor, it may make sense to set up your brokerage account after you've gained some experience with mutual fund switching and investing. Margin is best

reserved for more experienced investors. Options trading should be left for well-financed and very experienced traders. You can work your way to that as you gain experience. But because of the risk, it's not the place for a novice investor to get her feet wet in the early days of what should be a lifetime endeavor.

- **Preparing before trading.** Before you become a mutual fund switching or stock trading maven, put your money in the broker's money market account linked to your trading account. Think of the money market account as a place where you store your investing capital. Always mail your new contributions to this account, too. There is no hurry to start allocating money into the markets. If you must put some money to work right away, use small amounts and see how things go before making bigger bets. Do your homework and find the mutual funds or stocks that best match your long-term plans before allocating. Read the prospectus and online information at Morningstar.com and Yahoo! Finance. Don't be afraid to call the fund family or the broker and ask their phone reps questions. Don't make a move until you're sure that this is what you want to do.

- **Checking the market.** As a DIY investor, you have to put in the time to manage your own money. Get into the habit of checking the general trends of interest rates, the stock market, and the general financial and economic themes of the moment on a frequent basis. Pros do this daily. You may want to do it at least once or twice per week. Instead of checking your Facebook page with your morning coffee, go to CNBC, MarketWatch.com, or Yahoo! Finance and make sure that there is nothing ridiculous going on in the world that will have a negative impact on your portfolio that day.

- **What moves your money?** If you check the market, you should know what events mean to your portfolio. That means that you have to figure out how your mutual funds and stocks respond to what the market is doing. To get a feel for which index or market sector influences the price of your mutual funds, check the closing price of the index on a regular basis and compare the price change in your mutual fund to the activity in the index. Here is an example. Most growth funds tend to rise and fall in tandem with the Nasdaq Composite Index (COMPQ). If your growth fund does the opposite, meaning that it falls when Nasdaq rises, it may not be a good growth fund. Do this for all your funds. The more you perform these tasks, the better off you will be as an investor.

- **Develop contingency plans before things happen.** Aside from deciding how much money you will put into the markets and how often, you should think about what will make you take money out of your stocks or mutual funds. Thus, before you get started or as you go along, you should develop a plan that will allow you to act decisively if markets become volatile or prices start to drop aggressively.
- **Assume the worst.** What will you do if the Federal Reserve raises interest rates or the economy starts to shrink? Will you change your asset allocation? How will you change what financial assets you own? Will you set limits on your losses? If so, how much are you willing to lose before you cash in your chips? Will you buy more shares of your aggressive mutual fund when stocks fall and they take the fund's share price down with them? If so, how often will you buy these dips? What will you do if your Internet connection goes down and you know that the market is going to be volatile? You can develop your contingency and emergency plans with your financial planner or consultant. You can also read articles on these themes on the Internet. The important thing is to prepare yourself as best as possible for difficult times.

ALERT

Beware the talking heads on TV. Many so-called "experts" on financial television are there only to hawk their products, whether they are newsletters or asset management services. There are others who are actually worth listening to. If you watch financial television, get a good feel for who is worth listening to or not. And don't let the fancy credentials or the big brokerage association influence you. Check out what they say and find out for yourself whether they are trustworthy or not.

The Dangers of Online Investing

There are two basic problems with online investing. One is that it's so easy that you can spend all your time monitoring your portfolio. An even worse danger associated with this, especially when you are inexperienced, is that you may become impatient and make mistakes that will cost you money. The biggest problem is the potential for scams. Unfortunately, as you look for investment ideas, you may stumble upon websites that are dishonest and are just interested in taking your money. These websites may actually be criminal and only interested in stealing your identity and getting access to your financial information for personal gain. Even if they are not criminal, they may be interested in selling you access to information, which will not make you any money. This is especially true of websites that promise you wealth through penny stocks. These websites are known as phishing and "pump and dump" sites respectively. The bottom line is that if it sounds too good to be true, it is. Avoid the easy money lures and always do your homework.

Avoiding the Scammers

A great way to avoid scammers is to visit the SEC's website, *www.sec .gov*. Click on the "latest news" link and you'll find the agency's latest actions against scammers. There you will read about how criminals try to manipulate the system unscrupulously for their personal gain, and your losses. The website's enforcement link has a wealth of information about companies that are in violation of their required reporting to the SEC but are still being actively traded. These companies, in many cases, are actively promoted by so-called "market makers," which in fact may be stock promoters, or individuals who, via the Internet, but also through cold telephone calls, try to trick investors into buying shares of stocks that are still listed but have no businesses, no earnings, and haven't filed any kind of notice with the SEC to document the status of their current business.

What to Do if You Get Caught

Even if you read this book and are a cautious person, you may still get caught in a fraudulent scheme. If you get caught, or in the course of your research stumble onto a website that looks suspicious, you should contact your state's securities board or go to the SEC website's EDGAR section to see if the security is currently registered. You can also ask your state securities board if a person that has contacted you has a valid securities license in your state and whether there are any open complaints against her. Maybe the best thing is to assume the worst by considering any investments plugged on the Internet as being potentially fraudulent and sticking to mainstream investments.

If you need to contact the SEC, you can e-mail them at *help@sec.gov*.

What to Look for in an Investment Website

If you're going to be an online investor, it's a good idea to find good sources of information, ranging from those that provide actionable recommendations about what to buy and sell or how to allocate your portfolio, to those that provide good sound educational information that will make you a better investor. There are three basic types of websites that cater to investors: big portals like MarketWatch.com, brokerage websites that house your accounts, and subscription websites that provide detailed analysis, such as charts and editorial commentary, as well as buy and sell recommendations. To be sure, no one website will be appealing to everyone. Yet, the good ones, no matter what attracts you, should meet a basic set of criteria.

The Big Portals and Subscription Websites

Here are some important characteristics to look for in an information website:

- **Easy to use and access.** If it's not easy to navigate, you won't use it, no matter how good the information is.
- **News you can use and commentary that makes you think.** If a website is all about personalities and celebrities, it won't help you make money. Look for information that attracts you and that, if possible, makes something in your life or your investments more efficient, useful, and profitable, whether in time, money, or both.
- **Free real-time quotes and access to fundamental data for big portals.** If you're going to spend time reading an article, the site should have access to real-time quotes and access to basic financial data for the securities that it's discussing. Thus, if you find an interesting recommendation, you can start researching it immediately.
- **Good insightful analysis and easy-to-understand buy and sell recommendations for subscriber websites.** If the site provides recommendations and model portfolios, make sure that they list their results.

Your Account Website

Your broker's website should have some basic but very important features. They include:

- **Security.** An easy-to-access, password-activated, hacker-proof site with high-level security.
- **Ease of use.** Thus, it requires a trading screen that's easy to move through and that warns you when your order has errors.
- **Real-time quotes.** You don't trade stocks without the latest prices. Last hours' quotes may look good but are useless when you are ready to pull the trigger.
- **Versatility.** You should be able to trade stocks, mutual funds, ETFs, and bonds on the same website.
- **Immediate confirmations** should be available for your trades.
- **Real-time updates for your accounts.** You should know how much money you have every time you click that refresh button.
- **Customer service.** Access to 24-7 instant customer service, online, by chat, by phone, or all of the above, is a must.
- **Low minimum balance requirement.** This is a must for someone who is just getting started.
- **Access to special buy and sell orders** should be standard on your standard trading menu.
- **An automatic daily sweep** of any money that you don't have invested in the markets into a money market fund is essential.

ALERT

Beware the chat rooms. To be sure, a chat room may be a place where you can find out useful information. But it's also a place where scam artists operate. If you frequent chat rooms, always check out what you hear on your own. If it makes sense to use the information, go ahead. If it doesn't hold up to scrutiny, ignore it.

Useful Investment Websites

There are hundreds of investment websites. But there are only a few that offer something special that makes them stand out from the rest. Here is a list of very useful sites and what makes them different from the rest of the pack. This is not a ranking list, but it is meant to provide a cross section of sites and to give you a variety of ideas as to what is out there.

- **MarketWatch.com** (*www.marketwatch.com*). This is one of the original portals of online investing. Thus, it has stood the test of time. Aside from providing access to great information, such as company financials and real-time quotes, the editorial content, especially the analysis, opinion, and news reporting, is top-notch.
- **Investors.com** (*www.investors.com*). This website is the online presence of *Investor's Business Daily*. This site is all about trading and investing. You get a wealth of information about the stock market, individual stocks, futures, options, ETFs, and mutual funds. Their "Big Picture" column is as good a daily market recap as there is. The site has free content but may be worth a subscription.
- **Investing.com** (*www.investing.com*). This is a great website if you become interested in foreign currency trading. It has great access to global economic reports as they happen, although it focuses mostly on trading.
- **Yahoo! Finance** (*www.finance.yahoo.com*). This is a big portal similar to MarketWatch.com. The major difference is that much of the editorial content is linked from outside sources, although these are high-level sources. Real-time quotes, great financial research on companies, and general news are also available.
- **CNBC.com** (*www.cnbc.com*). Although CNBC has changed its format over the years, it's still the leader in business TV. Its website has interesting editorial content, which is more topic-focused and newsy than other financial websites. It also features commentary and reviews of important data from credible analysts with a proven track record.
- **E*TRADE** (*www.etrade.com*). This is a brokerage website where you may consider opening an account. It has excellent features for online investing and has been around for a long time.

- **Charles Schwab** (*www.schwab.com*). This is another brokerage website. Schwab is a pioneer in discount brokerage, and it caters to individual investors.
- **TD Ameritrade** (*www.tdameritrade.com*). Like other discount brokers, TD Ameritrade offers easy-to-use platforms and access to research information. TD Ameritrade also owns an analysis website that offers a great deal of financial information and tutorial services called *www.investools.com*.
- **The Motley Fool** (*www.fool.com*). The "Fool" specializes in making financial analysis and recommendations easy to understand. It's a good place to get comfortable with analysis and the markets overall.
- **Morningstar** (*www.morningstar.com*). This is a premier financial information site with special emphasis on mutual fund ratings and performance data. It's a great place to do your homework.

CHAPTER 18

Investment Taxes

Everyone has heard the line about taxes and death being inevitable. It's true, and investments are no exception. It's important to know that, unlike other forms of taxation, investment taxes can be managed with some flexibility. That means that before you invest, you should find a good CPA or tax expert to help you make the best possible choices in this area. And while no one likes to pay taxes, the other side of the coin is that in investing, if you pay taxes, it's a sign that you are making money.

How Taxes Affect Your Portfolio

When you become an investor, you will join the ranks of those who toil on one side or the other of a long-standing tug of war between Wall Street and the U.S. government. Wall Street fights hard to keep taxes on investment as low as possible. Uncle Sam wants a big chunk of it. So while your political preferences may lean one way or the other, the reality of it is that if you invest in a nonretirement account, you will pay taxes now. If you do most of your investing in an IRA, a 401(k) plan, or a similar retirement vehicle, you will pay taxes later.

The bottom line is that there is no point in fighting it. Instead, it's better to focus your efforts on learning about investment taxes and to figure out how to legally pay the least amount possible.

QUESTION

How big is the IRS?
According to data from 2014, the IRS requested just over thirteen billion, three hundred fifty-eight million dollars for its budget, while the number of employees had been falling into the high 90,000 range until 2013, when more hiring to police the Affordable Care Act added to the payroll of the agency.

In order to gauge what you are up against, it makes sense to, first, get a good handle on what kind of taxes you might face as an investor. Become familiar with capital gains taxes and investment income taxes. Once you get a good idea of these things, you should go talk to your accountant and see how you can make the best of the situation.

Although any investment may be taxed at some point, most often you will have to deal with taxes on your American stocks, bonds, and mutual funds, as well as the effect of your tax deferred strategies, such as your IRA, 401(k), and other retirement plans.

Types of Investment Taxes

There are three general ways in which the government taxes investments: through dividends, capital gains, and investment interest. Company profits are, at least partially, passed through to shareholders, who choose to receive them either as a payment or decide to have them reinvested in company shares through a dividend reinvestment plan (DRIP).

Capital Gains

A capital gain is what you receive when you sell a security, stock, bond, or other asset for a profit. Capital gains taxes differ based on how long you held the security prior to selling it. If you hold shares for less than a year, your capital gains are taxed at 35%, the same as normal income. If you make more than $400,000 a year, your short-term capital gains tax is 39.6%. Long-term capital gains, generated when you sell investments held longer than one year, are 0% to 20% depending on your income. Because some taxes related to the Affordable Care Act will be enacted over the next decade or longer, it makes sense to make sure that you consult your accountant as to whether any surprises are lurking in your tax future before you sell a large asset. If you have capital losses, you can use up to $3,000 per year to offset gains, and you can carry over current losses to future years.

ESSENTIAL

There is no substitute for keeping good, thorough, and accurate tax records. By carefully logging your investment confirmations, dividends, and related expenses, you could save yourself a bundle every tax year. The better the record, the better the chance of finding legal deductions.

Interest Income

Interest income and dividends are usually taxed at your marginal tax rate. This is the income that comes from interest-paying savings accounts, money market funds, and bond-related investments. A notable exception is the interest that you earn from tax-free municipal bonds at the state or federal level.

Two other important exceptions are the mortgage exemption and the exemption on your margin loans for investments. These deductions are based on your taxable investment earnings, and you usually can't include capital gains that are treated under the law or nontaxable interest or dividends. This may be something that you can discuss with your tax professional in detail.

Crafting Your Investment Tax Strategy

The two major goals of a sound strategy are to keep as much money as possible in your pocket as you can, and to do it legally. In other words, avoiding taxes within legal means is acceptable; evading taxes is illegal and can lead to major headaches and even bigger penalties if it is discovered. Your best chance of achieving success comes from thorough discussion of the topic with your tax and investment advisors.

FACT

You can't avoid taxes and death. But it is possible to avoid taxes in relation to death under certain circumstances. The benefits from a life insurance policy aren't taxable.

When planning your tax strategy, it makes sense to explore legal tax shelters. There are plenty of them written into the tax code, although the IRS and Congress are closing more of them as the U.S. government looks to reduce deficits. Use care when considering tax shelters, as enforcement action is increasing, especially when it comes to offshore accounts and similar vehicles. Keeping it simple is the best way to shelter your income. Consider your mortgage, business expenses, and oil, and if you're feeling a bit more sophisticated, you may want to look at oil and gas limited partnerships.

How to Measure Gains and Losses

If you had a tough year investing, the only positive is that it is likely that you will reduce your tax bill. On the other hand, if you had big gains, get ready to pay a fairly good-sized tax bill, unless you've done some planning ahead of time. Start to think about where things might end up in October. If you have some losing positions by this time, think about selling them by the end of the year in order to record some losses. Losses will trim your tax bill.

By the same token, if you've had a big loss, consider selling some of your winners. This may sound counterintuitive. But in fact, what you're doing is locking in more of your big gains, as the loss essentially hides your gain. The net effect is that your losses, by offsetting your gains, reduce the amount of taxes you would pay for the winners.

ALERT

Keep your eye out for foreign investment tax credits. Even if you don't own direct foreign investments, your international mutual fund may have paid taxes outside the United States. You can get credit for those taxes, or you can use them as part of your itemized deductions. Get the details from your CPA!

The most important aspect of tax planning is to have a measured approach. And don't forget that taxes are part of investing. By being aware of how you can reduce their effect on your portfolio's long-term growth, and by doing all the legal things that you can to get the benefits, you will go further. Finally, remember that you are investing, not tax planning. Your best tax plan won't do you a bit of good without good investments that actually make you money.

Know Your Holding Period

The holding period, how long you actually hold an investment, is what decides how much of a capital gain tax you will pay once you sell it. It's not complicated, a rarity in the tax code. If you hold an investment for more than one year before you sell it, you will incur a long-term capital gain tax, which is a lower tax rate. If you hold an investment for less than one year, your holding period is considered short-term and you will have a short-term capital gain bill on it. If you bought XYZ mutual fund on March 1, 2013, and sold it on March 1, 2014, it's a short-term holding period. If you sell it on March 2, 2014, or later, it's a long-term holding period, which means that you lower your tax bill by being patient.

Make the Most of Your Deductions

Many expenses related to your investment portfolio can be tax deductible. These can include phone calls to your broker or advisor, or any other expenses related to communication and fees. Here is a list of some of them:

- Trading account management fees
- Books, magazines, subscriptions to websites, investment newsletters, or investment courses that you read or participate in to improve your financial management skills
- Travel expenses to meet your financial advisor or for an investment course
- Fees related to record keeping of your investments, account setup fees for your IRA, or custodial fees

Methods for Reducing Your Tax Liability

Okay, there is no avoiding the paying of taxes on your investments. If you make money, the government makes money. But you can pay the least amount possible if you make plans before you invest. The key is to understand the ups and downs of your tax strategy and to relate them to the particular circumstances of any investment while coordinating the effect of the investments on your overall taxes. The following section provides some excellent guidelines to get you on the right side of the dreaded tax issue.

Stocks

In order to make sure that your tax liability is correct, you must keep the confirmation slips of your stock trades, especially if you've bought shares of the same company at different times. When you sell the stock, determine whether you have a gain or a loss by subtracting the cost basis of your stock (the amount you paid plus commission) from the sale price. You must also note the holding period, or the length of time you held the stock, in order to determine whether you will apply the long-term or the short-term capital gain rate to the sale.

Here is an example:

- Let's say you bought 100 shares of the fictitious Walla-Walla Corp. (WW) for $1,000 on January 2013, including the commission costs. Your basis is $10 per share.
- In March 2013 you bought another 100 shares of WW worth $2,000 including commission costs. This time your basis is $20 per share.
- You like Walla-Walla, and it continues to shine, so on January 2015 you buy another 100 shares for $3,000, including commission, bringing your basis to $30 per share.
- Walla-Walla continues to do well, but in October 2015 it hits $50 and you think it's time to take some money off the table, so you call your broker and tell him to sell 100 shares.

Without further instructions, he will follow the IRS guidelines of selling the first-in, first-out shares. Thus, your shares from January 2013 will go. If you tell him to sell a particular set of shares with a better tax advantage, he will do that. No matter which shares you sell, you will receive $5,000. The difference of your profit margin and your tax rate would come from the holding period. If you sell the January 2013 shares, your tax rate would be less since you held them for over two years (January 2013 to October 2015). That would give you a $4,000 long-term gain. The March 2013 shares would have a $3,000 long-term gain, while the January 2015 shares would bring you a $2,000 short-term gain.

Remember, your tax decisions should be based on your current needs if possible. If you have some short-term losses, you can use the short-term gains to offset them. If you don't have any transactions to offset, you can just use the long-term shares in order to pay the smallest amount of tax on this profitable trade. The key is to have this strategy thought out before you trade and to keep good records.

Mutual Funds

Mutual funds are a bit more complicated, as they have three different potential tax implications: dividend distributions, capital gains distributions, and gains or losses from selling of shares. Gains and losses from selling is the easiest to understand. If you sell shares for more than you paid for them, you will get a tax bill. If you lose money at the sale, you can use the loss, as you would with any other, to potentially offset a gain. Time factors for short-term or long-term holding periods are applicable as normal. You figure out the basis for your calculation as you do for stocks in the previous section.

Dividend distributions and capital gains distrubutions are a bit different. At some point during the year, often in the May-June and/or the November-December time frame for stock funds, and sometimes monthly or quarterly for bond funds, your mutual fund will pass on capital gains and dividend distributions. Dividend distributions, per share, result from the dividends that the mutual fund collects on its holdings. Capital gains distributions are the proceeds from the funds' profitable asset sales. As these are passed on to you, you have to report them on your tax bill even if you receive the distribution in shares that remain as part of your fund holdings.

FACT

The dividends from a municipal tax bond fund are usually not taxable. Also consider that if you are holding mutual funds, stocks, or any other investment that pays dividends or offers any other kind of distribution, these are tax-deferred, meaning that you don't pay taxes at the current rates. In that case, the distributions are best taken as shares of the mutual fund to increase your fund holdings.

Municipal Bonds

The interest on municipal bonds, because states and municipalities issue them, is exempt from federal income taxes, just as the interest from federal securities is exempt from local and state taxation. As a result, municipal bonds pay lower interest rates than bonds that are fully taxable, such as corporate bonds.

Unfortunately, municipal bonds are not 100% tax-free securities. That's because even though the interest is lower, any capital gains or losses that you receive when you sell them are taxed based on the same rules for other assets, including your tax bracket and the holding period. That means that if you sell munis for more than you paid for them, you will pay taxes. On the other hand, if you sell them for less, you will have a reportable tax loss and can use that to your advantage.

Life Insurance

Although term life insurance is a good thing to have, it has little benefit other than in death. However, there are other special types of life insurance policies that may be useful as investment and tax advantage vehicles for you. That's because by choosing a whole life, universal life, or single premium policy:

- You can save for retirement. Instead of paying only for insurance, part of your premium builds cash value. The IRS does not tax these investment premiums.
- You can borrow from your policy. Once your policy builds cash value, you can borrow from it, and you don't have to pay it back. If there are loans outstanding at the time of death, they are deducted from the insurance payoff to your beneficiaries. Interest due on the loan may also be paid via the policy's investment income.
- Although this is not advisable for routine expenses, if you have a financial emergency, it is possible to use the cash value of your insurance policy to cover it. If you are faced with this kind of significant choice, check with your insurance professional and your financial advisor before making this type of decision. The bottom line is that this may be a good alternative to have in your arsenal.

Annuities

Annuities are another popular insurance-investment hybrid with big tax advantages. Annuities are structured so that your heirs will inherit the amount of money that you have put into the policy, even if it's lost money. What makes annuities even more attractive is that, similar to IRAs and 401(k) plans, they allow you to save tax-deferred until you withdraw funds.

Think of an annuity as a tax-deferred mutual fund or CD. It rises in value, but you don't pay the taxes until you retire. At that time, you can take out a lump sum or receive payments periodically. An important point to remember is that while you can deduct your contributions into an IRA or other retirement plan, you can't deduct money you put into an annuity. The other thing to remember is that annuities are usually expensive to buy and have large surrender fees. They also have expense and mortality risks (risk based on your risk profile, age, health, and so on). There are also annual maintenance fees that tend to be higher than those charged by mutual funds.

ALERT

Beware the penalties. If you cash out your annuity before retirement age, you are likely to run into steep penalties, also known as surrender charges. The best way to avoid this is to look into the details before you buy. All annuities are not created equally, and even some in the same categories will have different charges and structures depending on the company that issues them. Furthermore, if you withdraw from the annuity before age 59½, the IRS will tag on a 10% penalty.

Understanding Legal Tax Shelters

Technically speaking, all the actions that you take to reduce your taxes, whether offsetting gains with losses or making maximal contributions to your IRA, among other things, are considered tax shelters. The goal is to shelter your income from being taken by the taxman, and you can accomplish this by deferring the tax bill (contributing to your retirement fund) or avoiding paying taxes completely. You can shelter taxable income in many vehicles, including investments and special investment accounts, and by using planning strategies that lower your current taxable income or offer favorable tax treatments.

A very useful tax shelter often overlooked by novice investors is real estate. It's the most popular tax shelter for one reason: the depreciation deduction you get on investment properties, especially rental properties. Depreciation is a calculation, on paper, that means that you don't have to pay for it right now. The good thing is that even though you don't pay for it, the deduction puts money in your pocket now, by reducing the money you pay in taxes.

ALERT

The IRS is always watching for tax evaders. So choose your shelters wisely. If they change the rules at some point in the future, you may be liable for both past and current taxes. It's a good idea to cut your tax bill legally. It's not a good idea to break the rules, as the penalties and the consequences could be very significant.

Novice investors also miss other useful tax shelters. Consider oil and gas investments, such as limited partnerships. They offer big deductions for drilling and exploration costs. The downside is that if the partnership does not find oil or gas, you will likely take some losses. This could leave you with some deductions but no income to offset them. Similar shelters include equipment leasing and cattle breeding–related partnerships. You will have to go through a specialist investment advisor to find these in most cases.

The easiest ways to shelter your money from taxes are to:

- Hold on to your investments for longer than one year to reduce the capital gains tax rate.
- Put as much money as possible in tax-deferred investments, such as IRAs, 401(k) plans, and college savings accounts.
- Maximize your itemized deductions by including your investment-related expenses.
- Above all, work closely with your tax professional to shelter the maximum without breaking the law.

By being aware of the tax consequences of your investments, by keeping good records, and by knowing the rules ahead of time, you can craft an excellent set of strategies that will keep more money in your pocket, legally.

CHAPTER 19

Investing for Education

With rising college tuition prices likely to remain in place over the foreseeable future, it's never too early to start saving so that your kids will have a chance at a good higher education. Fortunately, there are several investment options that will help you to save for this important event without sacrificing your retirement. You can invest in state-sponsored 529 plans or set up your own plan similar to an IRA. You can even do both. The most important thing is to look at all your options and get started as early as possible. Time goes by very fast.

Start Planning for College Tuition Now

There is only one take-home message in this chapter: Start saving for your kids' college tuition now before your options become limited. Even if you don't have children, start saving for their college tuition when you start thinking about having them. Starting early has one major benefit: Your savings will have a chance to grow faster through the power of compounding. College costs can run from $10,000–$15,000 per year to over $50,000, depending on the type of institution or whether it is a state or private school.

Sure, this sounds daunting, especially if you have very young children or are in the planning stages. However, there are some great tools that can help you get a handle on this and to organize your planning.

Enter the college planning tool that you can find at Sallie Mae, the government–private sector student loan agency (*www.salliemae.com*). Their College Planning Toolbox (*www.salliemae.com/plan-for-college/college-planning-toolbox*) is a great way to walk through college costs, letting you compare costs between thousands of public and private schools. The website also has excellent information regarding loans, grants, savings, and scholarships. Especially useful is the built-in assumption in all calculations that college costs will rise at the rate of 5% per year.

In order to point you in the right direction, Sallie Mae's tool asks you for the following:

- The current cost of attending the school of your choice
- The number of years before your child starts attending college
- The expected number of years your child will be attending college
- How much money you already have saved for college
- The expected rate of return on your investment

After you've completed the first step and get an idea as to how much you will need, the site offers suggestions as to how you can go about getting there, including scholarships, grants, loans, and other options.

Tax Sheltered Education Savings Plans

Until 2009, the taxman took a bite of any investments that you made to save for college. That changed with the American Opportunity Tax Credit program that lets you deduct a portion of your college costs under certain circumstances. The program is part of a set of initiatives that also allow you to grow college savings in a tax-deferred format and in some cases even without a tax bill. Consult your CPA for details as early as possible in the process, as these programs tend to be limited, expanded, or modified by Congress as time passes.

The key is that if you can grow your college nest egg in a tax-deferred format, you can save more and have better choices when it's time to spend the money. Think of this as a similar process to saving for retirement, except the need for the money may come sooner and the money may be spent faster. By using this tax-deferred format, you can keep more of your money for your designated use, your child's college tuition.

You have to do your homework because not all college savings programs offer significant tax advantages. However, the ones that do are tailored so that one or more of these factors apply. First, any money you put away now isn't taxed. Second, the earnings on your investment aren't taxable now. Third, the money doesn't get taxed when you withdraw it to pay for college.

The 529 Plans

Qualified tuition plans, known as 529 plans, offer significant tax advantages. These are state-sponsored plans that have revolutionized the college savings landscape. There are two categories: college savings plans, the most popular and commonly used type, and prepaid tuition plans.

The account holder, usually a parent or grandparent, sets up the account on behalf of the future student, also known as the beneficiary, and makes the investment decisions for the plan. These include investment choices, asset allocation, and risk management. There may be some limits on one or more of these functions depending on the particular state laws. When college arrives, you can use the money you've saved over the years to pay for "qualified higher education costs," including fees, books, and other expenses that meet the criteria in the state. The best aspect of 529 plans is that as long as you follow the rules and spend the money on what the plan allows, you won't have to pay federal income taxes. In most cases you won't have to pay state taxes either. Some states will give you current deductions and in some cases will give you a deduction if you contribute to any state's plan.

ALERT

Pay attention to what you spend your college savings plan money on. If you use it for expenses that don't qualify, you will receive a 10% penalty on top of the normal tax bill that you would receive. There is a lot of fine print in these plans when it comes to what is allowed and what may lead to penalties. Generally, though, key exclusions include computers (each college may be different on this), transportation, and certain room and board–related expenses, such as decorating a dorm room. You also can't deduct any expenses that you defer by using other college expense–related tax exemptions, such as the American Opportunity credit.

In some states you can get huge tax advantages, as the allowed contributions may be as large as $300,000. Another advantage is that there are no income limitations, which means that if you are in an upper income bracket, you can still take advantage of these plans. What's the catch? The contribution may be subject to the gift tax. As of the 2013 tax year, up to $14,000 per year was exempt from this rule. Even better, $70,000 deposited at one time could be used as a tax deduction if split over five years. This latter aspect of the plans offers the donor an opportunity to plan for tax advantages over a longer period of time. The $70,000 contribution can only be made once every five years, during which time no more contributions can be made to the plan. You can get more details at *www.savingforcollege.com*.

There are other limitations, too. For one, investment choices in 529 plans may be limited. Some states may offer only one or two mutual funds, while others may offer as many as thirty choices. Also, you can only switch investment choices once per year. Finally, the fact that you have a 529 plan reduces the amounts that you can qualify for in other forms of financial aid.

Coverdell Education Savings Accounts

Coverdell Education Savings Accounts (ESA) offer tax advantages and flexibility, as the money can be used for any education-related expenses, including primary, secondary, and college. The contributions are not tax deductible, but the earnings on the account are tax-free when you use them for allowable expenses.

ALERT

The downside to ESAs is that they can severely limit or completely eliminate the amount of financial aid that your child can be eligible for. This is because an ESA account is considered your child's asset. This type of item on a financial aid evaluation goes to the minus column with regard to what your child might need.

If an ESA makes sense, though, you would open the account at your local bank, brokerage, or other financial institution for each individual child. If you have three children, you would open three accounts, and so on. One child can have more than one ESA to her name.

Contributions are limited to $2,000 per child total. That means that if your child has three accounts, the $2,000 annual contribution must be split between the three accounts. Excesses, even if more than one party contributes them, will get you a tax penalty on any amount over the $2,000. You can't contribute to ESAs after the child turns eighteen, with the one exception being that you can contribute in the same year if you use the funds to pay for tuition. Of course, there are other limitations. Your contributions are limited based on your income. As of the 2014 tax year, individuals who make less than $95,000 or couples with $190,000 adjusted gross incomes could make the full $2,000 contribution per child. The contribution is phased out with $110,000 and $220,000 being the limit incomes for singles and couples. Finally, the benefits must be completely used by the time the beneficiary turns thirty years of age.

Although ESAs have their limitations, the advantages make them worth considering. Here are the three major ones:

- You can use the proceeds for any level of education: primary, secondary, or college.
- You can open the account anywhere you want, invest the ESA in any type of investment, stocks, or mutual funds, and control it in any way you wish.
- You can contribute to both 529 plans and ESAs as long as you understand the rules, keep good records, and plan for the tax consequences.

Prepaid Tuition Plans: Are They Worth It?

If you're one of those people who like to lock in future possibilities now, you may consider a prepaid tuition plan. You can do this through a prepaid tuition plan, which lets you pay now for tuition money that you will get later. All states have different quirks and nuances with this type of plan, which is covered under the 529 umbrella. The main difference between a prepaid tuition plan and a traditional 529 is that in the prepaid tuition plan, the parents or grandparents put money into a state-sponsored pool of money that is invested over time and that will pay for college tuition at participating state schools or at private or out-of-state schools with comparable costs, depending on the plan's stipulations and rules. The money you put in the plan today buys college tuition at today's prices and guarantees that price when it's time for the child to go to college, no matter what the cost is at that time. If you don't end up using the money, you can transfer it to another relative, or save it for grandchildren. In some cases you can get a full or partial refund. The downside is that these plans reduce your child's eligibility for financial aid, dollar for dollar. That means that if your child decides to go to a more expensive private school, you probably won't qualify for financial aid.

QUESTION

Where can I get detailed help on the specifics of my state plans?
The answer to this important question may be at the College Savings Plans Network (*www.collegesavings.org*). This website has both general and specific information about all the major college savings plans. More importantly, it can provide access to detailed information about individual college savings plans for each state.

Plans vary widely from state to state. For example, while all states offer full prepaid four-year college tuition plans, many let you pay for room and board costs. You may be able to choose a plan from another state if it is better at meeting your needs. So, which is the plan that is best for your family? Consider choosing a prepaid tuition college savings plan:

- If you don't like uncertainty
- If you lose sleep worrying about the future
- If your tax bracket and circumstances will disqualify your family from financial aid
- If the school your child wants to attend is covered by a prepaid plan

Finally, remember that if your prepaid plan doesn't cover all your costs, you can also set up an ESA. Between these two plans, you might put yourself in a better situation. Just because you have the two plans, you won't be upsetting any tax planning.

Education Bonds and CDs

Mutual fund–based 529 plans have had huge appeal during times in which the stock market has delivered high returns. But in the post–2008 market crash period, educational CDs and bonds have made a comeback. The fact is that these investments make sense for any market environment, because they offer you the opportunity for safety and portfolio diversification.

Education Bonds

Education bonds are issued by the U.S. Treasury and are similar to savings bonds. Specifically, education bonds must be issued after 1989 and are series EE or I bonds. These bonds are different in their tax treatment from regular savings bonds, as your interest earnings will usually be completely exempt from federal income tax. Here are the rules:

- You must use the bond proceeds, interest, and principal to pay for the qualified educational expenses in the same year that you redeem the bond.

- You can't buy these bonds unless you are at least twenty-four years of age.
- You have to register the bonds in your name if you plan on using them for your own educational expenses.
- If you plan on using them for your children's education, you must register them in your name or your spouse's name.
- If you're married, you won't get the tax benefit unless you file a joint return.
- Your child can only be registered as a beneficiary, not as a co-owner of the bond.

And, sure, there are more limits to consider. For example, as of 2013, the IRS phases out the deduction if you are a single taxpayer and make more than $72,850 to $87,850. For couples, the tax exclusion starts at $109,250 and is totally phased out above $139,250. These limits have been increasing since 2008, which makes for a nice trend and may make considering these bonds as a viable vehicle worthwhile if you are in a higher tax bracket. Always check with your CPA to see if there have been any changes in the trend. The U.S. Treasury website (*www.treasurydirect.gov*) is also a good place to look for the latest information.

College Certificates of Deposits

A certificate of deposit is a long-term bank deposit that pays you interest for the life of the deposit. Once you buy the CD, you can't withdraw it without a penalty, along with giving up the interest payments that remain over the life of the deposit. In the case of a college certificate of deposit, the idea is similar, with some wrinkles. You still deposit a lump sum of money for a specified period of time. There is still a penalty for early withdrawal. The difference is that the interest rate paid is a college-oriented rate based on the Independent College 500 Index (IC 500), an index created by the College Board, the same people that put the SAT together.

This is the big picture. The IC 500 rate is considered the benchmark for the inflation rate of college expenses. Banks then link the return on the education certificates of deposit to reflect the annual figure of the IC 500. Although there are some standards to govern these instruments, you should always check before you sign on the dotted line to make sure you understand how your bank "links" the rate of return on the CD to the IC 500. The good thing is that the IC 500 rate is the lowest rate that an educational CD will pay. The rate could be higher.

FACT

The Independent College 500 Index is compiled from the costs of full-time tuition, room and board, and fees from the nation's most expensive not-for-profit colleges. The index is published once per year and is a measure of the change in costs on a year over year basis with information compiled from the schools that compose the index. For example, in 2012–2013 the IC 500 was valued at $43,960. For 2013–2014 it was valued at $45,664, a 3.83% increase for the year. It's not a bad idea to check this out on a yearly basis at *http://professionals.college board.com.*

The actual method of using these CDs is pretty simple. Once you've made sure you read the fine print and have all the details ironed out, you buy "units." Each "unit" is the cost of one year's education. The minimum account to fund a "unit" is $500. You can buy the whole year at once or build it up over time, such as by using an automatic monthly savings plan. The beauty of the CD is that the money you deposit will grow at the same rate, or better, than the IC 500's year over year rate of change.

CHAPTER 20

Retirement Planning

It's never too early, or too late, to plan for retirement. If you have a choice, though, start early. The longer you save and invest, the more time your money has to compound, or grow based on its own gains. The reality is that the traditional blend of social security, company pension plans, and job security standards no longer apply. We are entering the era of skill, location, and professional portability, and to some degree volatility, where being well informed and able to make sound decisions will, more than ever, lead to success. This chapter is all about helping you hone your retirement planning skills and get ready to fund a big part of your own retirement through 401(k) plans and IRAs.

The Genius of Tax-Deferred Investing

Tax-deferred investing is so ingenious that it's hard to believe that Congress or the government had anything to do with it. In fact, it is nearly the complete opposite of everyday investing, where every dollar of profit made is fractured by taxes that must be paid to the government. Look at it this way: If you have a savings account that pays interest, at the end of every year, you give the government some of the interest as part of your tax bill. With a tax-deferred account, you still pay taxes. But you do so at a later predetermined time. The net effect is that your money builds up faster in the present, and you don't pay taxes on it until you withdraw it from the tax-deferred account.

FACT

A tax-deferred account is different from a tax-exempt account. The latter is an account in which you never pay taxes. A good example of a tax-exempt investment is the interest on a municipal bond. Remember that even tax-exempt investments may be taxable. If you sell a municipal bond for a profit, you still pay taxes on the capital gains.

The IRS will most likely tax the income and capital gains generated by your investments outside of tax-deferred accounts in the present. This general principle applies to stocks, bonds, mutual funds, and real estate. Even businesses and niche investments, such as collectables, where you can make money or are at risk of losing money, will generally have a date with the taxman.

Thus, the allure of tax-deferred investments is that you can delay paying taxes, as long as you don't withdraw the money from the account. Even better is the fact that contributions to tax-deferred investments are tax deductible, partially or completely, now. To be sure, there are some notable exceptions, such as Roth IRAs or deductions that are phased out for higher-income taxpayers. The downside is that early withdrawal from these accounts sets you up to pay some hefty penalties that really eat into the amount of money that you withdraw. In fact, most experts worth their salt will tell you that it's just not worth it to withdraw from a tax-deferred account.

ALERT

Beware of neglecting your retirement accounts. Too many people put money into their IRA or 401(k) plans and don't bother to look at what's happening to their nest egg. Just because it's a long time from the present to the time when you will need the money, and even though stocks tend to rise over long periods of time, you should apply the traditional principles of investing to your retirement plan. That means paying attention to your asset allocation, monitoring your returns with regard to how the markets are acting, and making sure that the accounting and the fees are correct and fair.

Finally, the money you put into tax-deferred accounts, such as 401(k) plans and IRAs, is pretax money. That means that the money is deducted from your taxable income, so not only do you not pay taxes on the money you put into the account, but your overall taxable income is reduced. To get more information on your marginal income tax rate and your maximal contribution to tax-deferred accounts, check out the IRS website (*www.irs.gov*).

It's Never Too Early to Start

This is not a deeply scientific or philosophical question. The earlier you start investing, the more time you will have to maximize the amount you have when it's time to retire. It's really a simple concept; you want to give your money the most time possible to become as large a sum as possible. Think about all the potentially crazy things that can happen in a lifetime. There will be economic booms and busts. There will be periods of dramatic changes in technology. And there will be wars, climate events, and periods of personal difficulties. The bottom line is that starting early gives your money more time to ride the ups and downs, and to recover from any significant surprises.

Let's say that you have two twenty-five-year-olds in similar jobs with similar earnings and similar access to a 401(k) plan. Ellie decides that she is going to start out right away, so she socks $2,000 per year into her plan for ten years, until she's thirty-five, and then never invests again. Rory waits until he's thirty-four before he gets started. He puts $2,000 in his plan for thirty years, and saves three times as much as Ellie. If they both earn 10% per year on average until they retire, Ellie ends up with $556,197 while Rory ends up with $328,988. That's because Ellie started earlier and let the markets compound her way to a better retirement fund. They both did a nice job of saving. And they both ended up in better shape than many. But the numbers speak for themselves. The moral of the story is that by starting out early, you can end up in a much better place. To get an idea as to how compounding may work for you, visit *http://finance.toolkit.com*.

The 401(k) Plan

These hybrid DIY retirement plans have been around long enough now to have stood the test of time. 401(k) plans are set up by employers, and have largely replaced traditional pension plans, essentially shifting the burden of retirement, at least partially, to employees. If you use them correctly, by getting started, investing in them early, and staying connected to their progress, you can do quite well and have a tidy little, or big, nest egg by the time you call it quits from your job. Your company will give you a list of options where you can invest, and the money is pooled and invested into stocks, mutual funds, bonds, or other investments.

Here are some significant reasons not to miss an opportunity to start contributing to your 401(k):

- The money you save in the plan is earmarked for your retirement and is deducted from your pretax dollars.
- You get a tax deduction, and you don't pay taxes on the money in the plan until you take it out in the future.
- Employers usually match your contribution partially, as much as 10%, 25%, or even 50% of what you contribute. That means that just by the act of making your contribution, you trigger some free money into your account. The bottom line is that your employer's matching contribution is helping the growth rate of your investment at no charge to you.
- Because the money is in a retirement account, you won't get at it easily before it's time, and neither will the IRS. That means that it will have the best chance to grow and be there when you need it.

There is, as always, a downside. If you take the money out before a set date, usually age 59½, the IRS will whack you with a hefty penalty. And as always, it's very important to know where the money is being invested and to keep tabs on what kind of return the plan is delivering.

Your 401(k) Investing Strategy

Retirement investing is all about the long term. That means that it's not as important to worry about weekly or monthly changes in the stock or bond market. But at the same time, there is no excuse for neglecting your nest egg and avoiding important decisions as they arise. The most important thing is to keep adding money to your account in regular intervals. The investment approach known as dollar cost averaging, where you put the same amount of money into the plan in regular intervals, monthly or quarterly, is ideal for this kind of plan. But it is also important to adhere to your risk profile and to follow good investment discipline as you would in any other investment.

That means that you should make sure that you know how each of the investment choices in the plan is working at any one time. And don't be afraid to make changes from one class of investment to another over time in order to get better returns or reduce risk, depending on the long-term trends of the markets. In other words, a 401(k) is no different than other investments when it comes to your responsibilities. Especially dangerous may be the investment option available to some 401(k) investors, where the employing company's own stock is the major investment vehicle for the plan. If this is the case, the plan is only as good as the company's stock at any one time. If your company is faring well, your retirement is likely to do well during the period. But if things are not going well, such as if your company is in danger of bankruptcy or is having legal trouble, your retirement may be in jeopardy. It's not necessarily a bad thing to have some company stock in your 401(k), especially if that's how your employer contributes its portion to your plan. Think of that as free money. Just make sure that company stock is not the major portion of your investment or the only asset in your 401(k).

You Can Take It with You

You can't take your money when you die. But you can, and should, take your 401(k) plan with you when you change companies or become self-employed. If your new employer has a 401(k), you can have your current plan transferred or rolled over to a new account. Rolling it over, or having it directly transferred from one trustee to another, will save you 20% that would be levied on the money if you take possession of the money in the plan yourself. If you take possession of the money but don't re-establish it as a retirement plan with your new employer, you'll get hit with more taxes and penalties. Another negative is the fact that if you take possession and then restart the 401(k) elsewhere, you need to come up with the 20% that your old employer took out from your own pocket. If you become self-employed, then turn your 401(k) into an IRA. No matter what you do, make sure that you avoid taking possession of the money yourself, and that you make all the rollovers, transfers, and establishing of new accounts within sixty days of starting the process.

Taking Money Out of a 401(k) Plan

This is tricky. Because 401(k) plans allow you to borrow from them, it's tempting to use them as piggy banks to fund down payments for a new home, or maybe to buy a sports car. Still, in most cases, you're just asking for trouble when you take out money tagged for retirement for short-term uses. To be sure, if you are facing a life or death situation, such as your house is near foreclosure or you're hit with some unforeseen medical expenses, and you have no other means of getting through, your 401(k) is fair game, but not without cost. Early withdrawals are expensive, as you will have to pay the full tax bill on the money you take out, and a 10% penalty.

There is one loophole that could save you a big tax and penalty hit. If you borrow from your 401(k) plan under certain circumstances, you may not incur penalties or tax consequences if you follow the rules. However, and you knew this was coming, there is a catch. You have to pay back the loan in full before you stop working for the employer who maintains the plan.

Here are the rules of engagement under normal circumstances: You can take distributions (withdraw money) from your plan without penalties starting at age 59½, whether you are retired or not. By the time you turn 70½, you have to take out the minimum required distribution.

Individual Retirement Accounts (IRAs)

IRAs are immensely popular because they allow you to save for retirement while deferring taxes, are very flexible in what you can use for investment vehicles, and come in two basic types: traditional and Roth. An even nicer touch is that in 2005, the Supreme Court ruled that IRAs are fully protected from creditors if you need to file for personal bankruptcy.

Traditional IRAs

The good thing about IRAs is that over the past ten years, Congress has been making it more attractive to save for retirement through IRAs. For example, in 2008 your maximum contribution was $5,000. In the 1990s, the maximum that you could put in a traditional IRA was $2,000. Now, in 2013 and 2014 you could contribute $5,500, or $6,500 if you were above age fifty, to your IRA. Married spouses can contribute to individual IRAs if they file jointly, even if only one spouse works. Contributions may be tax deductible depending on the situation and the current state of the rules, which do change from time to time. Your contribution can't exceed your taxable compensation for the year. You can find easy-to-use IRA contribution calculators at *http://finance.toolkit.com*. Go to "Tools for Retirement Planning" and you will find worksheets, sample tax forms, financial calculators, and other useful information to help you get started.

QUESTION

Can I save for retirement if I work part-time?
According to the IRS, in 2013, an "unmarried college student working part-time" and "earning $3,500 per year" could contribute $3,500 to an IRA. The best part about it is that the IRS allows "Danny's grandmother" to make the contribution on his behalf.

As with 401(k) plans, you can start withdrawing your money at 59½, and you must start withdrawing the minimum out of the account by the time you reach 70½. You will pay taxes at the current tax rate when you make your withdrawal, but only on the amount that you withdraw. And here is a bonus:

Your income level, even if you work part-time, is likely to drop when you retire. That will likely put you into a lower tax bracket.

You can start your IRA through a bank, a brokerage house, or a mutual fund family. Because there is stiff competition for your business, you should look for a no-fee IRA. Those are easy to find through the big mutual fund families and brokerages. Banks tend to offer fewer options, and may have higher fees. And with a mutual fund or brokerage firm, you will have a greater opportunity to tweak your asset allocation and to manage your portfolio according to market conditions and your risk profile. Don't be too passive with this money. Consider taking some risks, if it suits your risk profile. But always be aware that with unmanaged risk you could incur big losses. As a general rule, keeping an eye on your IRA on a weekly, monthly, or quarterly basis makes more sense than minding the store every five years. There is no substitute for knowing what you need to know when you need to know it.

Roth IRAs

These IRAs have been around since 1998, and they offer a different approach to retirement savings. Because you pay the taxes on the contributions as you add the money to the account, you don't pay taxes when you make withdrawals. Your contributions are also not tax deductible as with traditional IRAs. The benefits of the Roth accounts are simple:

- You don't have to pay taxes when you withdraw the money.
- There is no minimum distribution requirement.
- If you don't withdraw the money, you can pass the account to your heirs tax-free when you die.

Generally, the contribution limits are similar to those for traditional IRAs. However, they are subject to income levels, and they are subject to change. It's a good idea to get advice from your CPA or visit the IRS website (*www .irs.gov*) for the latest information. In 2013, the eligibility for Roth IRA contributions was phased out between $112,000 and $178,000, based on your modified adjusted gross income and your filing status. For 2014, the range was between $114,000 and $181,000. In comparison, in 2008 the limits were between $101,000 and $159,000.

You can roll over money from a traditional IRA to a Roth account, but you should check with your tax advisor and make sure that it's a good idea to do so based on your current financial situation. If you can't deduct your current contributions but still have money available to save for retirement, you may want to use the Roth option, if you are eligible. Roth IRAs also make sense if you expect higher tax rates upon your retirement or if you think you might need that money before you retire. If you are uncertain about the future of tax rates, or the unknown keeps you from getting sleep, a Roth IRA may make sense for you.

If you decide to make the switch to a Roth, you can start by asking your current IRA custodian about your next step. They will provide you with a good analysis of your situation and send you the correct forms. Your CPA will also help. Make sure that you are well informed and comfortable before making the switch.

To Roth or Not to Roth: Which Makes the Most Sense?

The answer to the proverbial Roth IRA question depends on whether paying taxes now or later makes the most sense for you. And, as with everything else financial, what you do depends on your individual financial situation and expectations for the future. You can calculate your heart away. And you can research this until you are blue in the face or have carpal tunnel syndrome from punching your smartphone, tablet, or PC keyboard looking for answers. Your CPA is also likely to generate some fees based on your query, while likely making the most sense as a source of assistance.

But here is the real answer: No one knows what lies ahead over the next thirty years. Politics, your health, and the general chaotic nature of the universe will play their roles and influence what happens, despite your best guess and thorough research. The bottom line may be this simple: Whether you choose a traditional or a Roth IRA, you are making a good decision because you have decided to save for your retirement. So do your homework, talk to your accountant, and jump.

Health Savings Accounts (HSAs)

The Affordable Care Act changed everything with regard to health care. Even if the law is modified in the future, it is likely that higher deductibles and out of pocket expenses will remain, along with higher health-care costs due to the changing demographics of the United States resulting from the aging of the Baby Boomers. You should also consider the fact that Medicare benefits, disability requirements, and other forms of assistance, such as Medicaid, are also likely to change, probably toward the side of being less generous. That's why it makes sense to consider a health savings account.

Here are the basic facts:

- With an HSA you can save money for your health expenses, much as you would save for retirement via an IRA or a 401(k) plan.
- You must have a high deductible health-care plan, with no other health coverage.
- Generally, the higher the deductible, the more you can save in an HSA.
- You can manage your HSA in a similar fashion to your IRA, and the money and the compounded earnings that you don't use will be there until your death.
- You must not be enrolled in Medicare. That means that you can no longer contribute to your HSA once you enroll in Medicare.
- If you die, your beneficiary receives the money in your HSA. If the beneficiary is your spouse, the HSA becomes your spouse's HSA. If your beneficiary is someone else, he will pay taxes on the money in the HSA for the current tax year.
- You must not be listed as a dependent on someone else's tax return.

There are some different rules for employers, employees, and the self-employed with regard to HSAs. And there are likely to be some changes to these general requirements in the future as the health-care system dynamics change. You can get the most current details by reviewing Publication 969 from the IRS. There is also useful general information at the U.S. Treasury's website, *www.treasury.gov.*

Time and Focus Are Your Best Allies

There is an old saying that goes: "Youth is wasted on the young." Nonsense. That's just sour grapes from old people who have wasted their time. Youth, especially when it comes to retirement planning, is a blessing and an opportunity. That's because time is on your side and because, if you stay focused, you can learn from your mistakes and have the time to show that you have learned from them.

Here are some things that you can do and that will serve you well over time. Take advantage of all your tax-deferred opportunities. If you can invest in an IRA and a 401(k) simultaneously, do it. Even if you can't deduct both of your contributions, they will still grow tax-deferred. Plan for the worst-case scenario. Plan your retirement as if Social Security will not exist when you turn sixty-five. It will probably still be there. But if you've planned for the worst, you will make a better effort and be in a better position. Sometimes it pays to worry and plan ahead. This is one of those times.

Online and Discount Brokers

Included are the largest, most accessible discount and online brokers in the United States. The list is meant to help you get started quickly in your DIY investing. The list is purposely tilted toward the largest brokers because they tend to have the best online platforms, 24-7 support to go along with great, easy-to-read tutorials, as well as well-trained reps that can help you get started or answer questions as you progress.

Charles Schwab

www.schwab.com

800-435-4500

High volume and low prices from one of the biggest of the brokerage houses. Local branches located throughout the United States.

E*TRADE Financial

www.etrade.com

800-786-2575

High volume, very popular site with low prices. Walk-in branches in several states.

Fidelity

www.fidelity.com

800-544-6666

Recently rated best online broker by Kiplinger. Many investor centers located throughout the United States.

Scottrade

www.scottrade.com

800-906-7268

Has more than 400 walk-in branches throughout the United States.

ShareBuilder

www.sharebuilder.com

866-590-7629

A service of Capital One.

TD Ameritrade

www.tdameritrade.com

800-669-3900

More than 100 local branch offices nationwide.

USAA Brokerage Services

www.usaa.com

800-531-8343

Services are offered to current and former military personnel and their families.

Vanguard Brokerage Services

www.vanguard.com

800-992-8327

Vanguard Brokerage Services, unlike Vanguard mutual funds, doesn't mind if you trade in and out of securities.

Investment Publications

The Internet is full of websites that will provide you with excellent information. Some will give you big ideas, while others will help you to make investment decisions. As always, consider your risk profile, your long-term goals, and your willingness to spend time tending to your investing program before you make any buy or sell decisions. This group of websites is a very good set of places to get started.

Subscription prices listed are those posted on the publications' websites as of July 2014 and may represent special or limited-time offers. To help you decide which publications are the most useful to you before you shell out the money for a long-term subscription, visit your local library. Among other resources, you can gain valuable insight about investing from the following:

The *Wall Street Journal*

Published by Dow Jones and Company, the *Wall Street Journal* is a leading global newspaper with a focus on business. Founded in 1889, the newspaper has grown to a worldwide daily circulation of more than 2 million readers. In 1994, Dow Jones introduced the *Wall Street Journal Special Editions*, special sections written in local languages that are featured in more than thirty leading national newspapers worldwide. The *Wall Street Journal Americas*, published in Spanish and Portuguese, is included in approximately twenty leading Latin American newspapers. The *Wall Street Journal* offers digital-only subscriptions for $24.99 per month, and a combination digital and print subscription for $28.99 per month.

800-568-7625
www.wallstreetjournal.com

Barron's

Barron's is also known as the *Dow Jones Business* and *Financial Weekly*. With its first edition published in 1921, *Barron's* offers its readers news reports and analyses on financial markets worldwide. Investors will also find a wealth of tips regarding investment techniques. One-year print plus online subscriptions are $100.94, and a one-year online-only subscription costs $100.94.

800-975-8620
www.barrons.com

Investor's Business Daily

Founded in 1984, *Investor's Business Daily* is a newspaper focusing on business, financial, economic, and national news. The publication places a strong emphasis on offering its readers timely information on the stock market and stock market–related issues. The front page of each issue provides a brief overview of the most important business news of the day. It's published five days a week, Monday through Friday, and you can get a one-year subscription for $329, which includes full access to its website. The strictly online edition, called eIBD, offers annual subscriptions for $269 or monthly subscriptions for $28.95 per month. A one-year subscription to the daily print edition and eIBD is $389.

800-459-6706
www.investors.com

Forbes

Forbes magazine is a biweekly business magazine for "those who run business today—or aspire to." Each issue contains stories on companies, management strategies, global trends, technology, taxes, law, capital markets, and investments. A one-year subscription, or twenty-six issues, is currently discounted 87% and only costs $20, and that comes with complete access to its real-time website.

800-888-9896
www.forbesmagazine.com

Money

Money is a monthly personal finance magazine from Time-Warner publications, covering such topics as family finances, investment careers, taxes, and insurance. Each issue includes tips, advice, and strategies for smart investing. The magazine also features other related matters like finding cheap flights, buying a home, and preparing for tax season. It also offers a substantive annual mutual fund guide. A one-year subscription, or thirteen issues, is $14.95.

800-633-9970
http://time.com/money

Bloomberg BusinessWeek

This weekly publication comes jam-packed with comprehensive coverage of both the U.S. and global business scene. From the economy to politics to how both impact stock prices, *Bloomberg BusinessWeek* provides in-depth market analysis and incisive investigative reporting. A twelve-week print, mobile, and tablet subscription costs $9, and a fifty-week print, mobile, and tablet subscription is $40.

888-878-5151
www.businessweek.com

Fortune

Every month, *Fortune* magazine, a Time-Warner publication, offers analysis of the business marketplace. The publication's annual ranking of the top 500 American companies is one of its most widely read features. *Fortune* has been covering business and business-related topics since its origins in 1930. A one-year "All Access" subscription, which includes twenty issues, is $19.99.

800-621-8000
www.fortune.com

Kiplinger's Personal Finance

One of the most respected names in financial publications, Kiplinger offers investing ideas, updates on companies, insider interviews with top financial experts and fund managers, and very detailed listings of the best-performing mutual funds in a wide range of categories. One-year subscriptions cost $12 for either the print or digital edition.

800-544-0155
www.kiplingers.com

Value Line Investment Survey

A weekly publication available at most libraries and through subscription, it offers ratings, reports, opinions, and analysis on about 130 stocks in seven or eight industries on a weekly basis. Approximately 1,700 stocks in about ninety-four industries are covered every thirteen weeks. CD-ROM subscribers can also purchase an expanded version containing reviews of 5,000 stocks. A thirteen-week trial subscription, which includes full online access, costs $75; a one-year subscription costs $598.

800-634-3583
www.valueline.com

Glossary of Terms

Investing has a language all its own, but it doesn't have to be intimidating. The average investor only needs to know the basics, so if you have an understanding of the terms in this glossary, you're off to a good start.

annuity

A contractual financial agreement between you and an issuing company. You give the issuing company a certain amount of money, and in turn the company promises to invest your money and repay you according to the option or payment method that you choose.

arbitrage

The practice of taking advantage of the difference in price of the same security traded on two different markets. For instance, if Nortel Networks were trading at $100 (U.S.) on the Toronto exchange and $99 on the NYSE, an arbitrageur would buy shares on the NYSE and sell them on the Toronto exchange.

asset

Anything you own that has monetary value, including cash, stocks, bonds, mutual funds, cars, real estate, and other items.

asset allocation

The specific distribution of funds among a number of different asset classes within an invest-ment portfolio. Investment funds may be split among a number of different asset classes, such as stocks, bonds, and cash funds, each of which has unique risk and return characteris-tics. Determining just how to allocate funds depends on the financial plans of the individual investor.

average daily volume

The average number of shares traded per day over a specified period.

bankruptcy

A legal process where a party acknowledges that he is unable to pay his debts, and makes arrangements for those debts to be legally (if not financially) settled. The party declaring bankruptcy either allows his assets to be sold to repay creditors to the extent possible (liquida-tion bankruptcy), or works with the court to set up a plan to pay all or some of his debt over a period of several years (reorganization bankruptcy).

bear

Someone who believes that the securities market(s) or a specific security will decline in value.

bear market

A market in which a group of assets (normally securities) falls in price or loses value over a period of time. A prolonged bear market may result in a decrease of 20 percent or more in market prices. A bear market in stocks may be due to investors' expectations of economic trends; in bonds, a bear market results from rising interest rates.

beneficiary

A person (or other entity, like a charitable foundation) who is named in a legal document (like a will or a trust agreement) to receive specific assets or to have the right to use specific assets.

beta

A statistical calculation that compares a security's volatility to a benchmark, usually the S&P 500 Index for stocks, for example. A beta greater than 1 means the security is more volatile than the index. For instance, a beta of 1.5 means the security is historically 50 percent more volatile than the index.

bid price

The price a prospective buyer is ready to pay for a security. The term is commonly used by traders who stand ready to buy or sell security units at publicly quoted prices.

blue chip

A term used to describe companies that have established themselves as reliably successful over time, often by demonstrating sound management and creating quality products and services. Such companies have shown the capability to function in both good and bad economic times, and usually pay dividends to investors even during lean years. Most blue chips are large cap, *Fortune* 500–type stocks like IBM or General Electric.

bonds

Loans from investors to corporations and governments given in exchange for interest payments and timely repayment of the debt. Interest rates are usually fixed.

bottom-up analysis

The search for outstanding performance of individual stocks before considering the impact of economic trends. Such companies may be identified from research reports, stock screens, or personal knowledge of the products and services.

budget
A detailed listing of income and expenses by category, usually prepared with an eye toward the future. Used by households and businesses alike to gain a tighter control over incoming and outgoing cash.

bull
Someone who believes that the securities market(s) or a particular security will increase in value.

bull market
An extended period of rising securities prices. Bull markets generally involve heavy trading, and are marked by a general upward trend in the market, independent of daily fluctuations.

capital gain
The appreciation in the value of an asset that occurs when its selling price is greater than the original price for which the asset was bought. The tax rate on capital gains depends on how long the asset was held, and is often lower than the rate on ordinary income.

capital gain distributions
Payments to the shareholders of a mutual fund based on profits earned from selling securities in the fund's portfolio. Capital gain distributions are usually paid once a year.

certificate of deposit (CD)
Money deposited with banks for a fixed period of time, usually between one month and five years, in exchange for compound interest, usually at a fixed rate. At the end of this term, on the maturity date, the principal may either be repaid to the depositor or rolled over into another CD. Any money deposited into a CD is insured by the bank (up to FDIC limits), making these very low-risk investments. Most banks set heavy penalties for early withdrawal of monies from a CD.

closed-end fund
A mutual fund where investors trade shares on an exchange, rather than buying shares from and redeeming them with the fund itself. Share price is determined by supply and demand for fund shares (as opposed to net asset value for regular mutual funds, also called open-end funds).

commission

A fee charged by a stockbroker (and, in some cases, a financial advisor) who executes securities trade transactions for an investor. This fee is generally a percentage based on either the number of shares bought or sold or the value of the shares bought or sold.

compound interest

Interest earned on the original investment (or deposit) amount plus any previously earned interest; effectively new interest is paid on already-earned interest. This helps the investment grow more quickly than it would with simple interest, which is applied only to the original investment amount.

cost basis

The total original purchase price of an asset, which may include items other than just the asset price, such as sales tax, commissions, and delivery and installation fees. This total amount is subtracted from the sale price of the asset to compute the capital gain or loss when that asset is eventually sold.

creditor

Any person (or entity) to whom you owe money.

credit risk

The risk that the principal you've invested through debt securities (like bonds) will not be repaid at all or on time. If the issuer of a debt security fails to repay the principal, the issuer is deemed to be in default.

default

To fail to repay principal or make timely payments on a bond or other debt investment security as promised. More likely to happen with high-yield corporate bonds (a.k.a. junk bonds) than other types of bonds.

defined-contribution retirement plan

A retirement plan offered by employers that allows employees to contribute to the plan but does not guarantee a predetermined benefit at retirement. Rather, the amount of the contribution is predetermined by the employee, typically as a percentage of pay. Examples of such plans include 401(k), 403(b), 457, and profit-sharing plans.

discount broker

Brokerage firms that offer cut-rate fees for buying and selling securities, usually online or over an automated tele-service, although some also offer fax trade order options. Among the most prominent are Charles Schwab and TD Ameritrade.

diversification

The process of optimizing an investment portfolio by allocating funds to a number of different assets. Diversification minimizes risks while maximizing returns by spreading out risk across a number of investments. Different types of assets, such as stocks, bonds, and cash funds, carry different types of risk. For an optimal portfolio, it is important to diversify among assets with dissimilar risk levels. Investing in a number of assets allows for unexpected negative performances to balance out with or be superseded by positive performances.

dividend

A payment made by a corporation to its shareholders that represents a portion of the profits of the company. The amount to be paid is determined by the board of directors, and dividends may be paid even during a time when the company is not performing profitably. Dividends are paid on a set schedule, such as quarterly, semiannually, or annually. Dividends may be paid directly to the investor or reinvested into more shares of the company's stock. Even if dividends are reinvested, the individual is responsible for paying taxes on the dividends earned. Mutual funds also pay dividends, from the income earned on the underlying investments of the fund portfolio. Dividends usually are not guaranteed (except with certain types of preferred stock) and may vary each time they are paid.

dividend yield

The current or estimated annual dividend divided by the market price per share of a security. Used to compare dividend-paying shares of different corporations.

dividend reinvestment plan (DRIP)

A plan allowing investors to automatically reinvest their dividends in the company's stock rather than receive them in cash. Many companies waive the sales charges for stock purchased under the DRIP.

Dow Jones Industrial Average (DJIA)

An index to which the performance of individual stocks or mutual funds can be compared; it is a means of measuring the change in stock prices. This index is a composite of 30 blue-chip companies ranging from AT&T and Hewlett-Packard to Kodak and Johnson & Johnson. These 30 companies represent not just the United States; rather, they are involved with commerce on a global scale. The DJIA is computed by adding the prices of these 30 stocks and dividing by an adjusted number that takes into account stock splits and other divisions that would interfere with the average. Stocks represented on the Dow Jones Industrial Average make up between 15 percent and 20 percent of the total market.

due diligence
An in-depth examination of a company's business prospects. Used by investors to analyze prospective investments.

earnings growth
A pattern of increasing rate of growth in earnings per share from one period to another, which usually causes a stock's price to rise.

equity
Equity is the total ownership or partial ownership of an asset minus any debts that are owed in relation to that asset (like a home with a mortgage). Equity also refers to the amount of interest shareholders hold in a company as a part of their rights of partial ownership. Equity is considered synonymous with ownership, a share of ownership, or the rights of ownership.

escrow
Money or other assets held by an agent until the terms of a contract or agreement are fulfilled. For example, many mortgage companies require borrowers to pay prorated property taxes monthly along with their mortgage payments; these funds are held in an escrow account until payment is due to the local government.

exchange-traded mutual fund (ETF)
An investment pool, similar to a mutual fund, whose shares trade over an exchange much like shares of stock. Most ETFs mirror a benchmark index, holding the securities tracked by that index.

financial advisor
A financial planning professional (typically licensed and accredited) who helps people manage their wealth. Functions may include preparing a retirement savings plan, devising tax strategies, and preparing an estate planning strategy, among other financial services.

fiscal year

Any 12-month period designated by a business as its accounting year. Once declared, a company's fiscal year does not change, unless it makes a formal change approved by the IRS.

foreclosure

A legal process that terminates an owner's right to a property, usually because the borrower defaults on payments. Home foreclosures usually result in a forced sale of the property to pay off the mortgage.

forex

Foreign currency exchange markets.

fundamental analysis

An analysis of a company's current and past balance sheets and income statements used to forecast its future stock price movements. Fundamental analysts consider past records of assets, earnings, sales, products, management, and markets in predicting future trends of a company's success or failure. By appraising a company's prospects, these analysts assess whether a particular stock or group of stocks is undervalued or overvalued at its current market price.

going public

When a company that has previously been wholly privately owned offers its stock to the general public for the first time.

good for the day

Buy or sell limit order that will expire at close of trading if not executed.

good until canceled

Buy or sell limit order that remains active until canceled.

growth investing

An investment style that emphasizes companies with strong earnings growth, which typically leads to stock price increases. Growth investing is generally considered more aggressive than "value" investing.

hedge
Hedging is a strategy of reducing risk by offsetting investments with investments of opposite risks. Risks must be negatively correlated in order to hedge each other—for example, pairing an investment with high inflation risk and low immediate returns with investments with low inflation risk and high immediate returns. Long hedges protect against a short-term position, and short hedges protect against a long-term position. Hedging is not the same as diversification; it aims to protect against risk by counterbalancing that specific area of risk.

individual retirement account (IRA)
A retirement account that anyone who has earned income can contribute to. Amounts contributed to traditional IRAs are usually tax-deferred. Amounts contributed to Roth IRAs are not currently deductible but taxes are never levied on the earnings.

inflation
A general increase in prices coinciding with a fall in the real value of money, as measured by the Consumer Price Index.

inflation risk
The risk that rising prices of goods and services over time will decrease the value of the return on investments. Inflation risk is also known as purchasing-power risk because it refers to increased prices of goods and services and a decreased value of cash.

intrinsic value
A term favored by value-oriented fundamental analysts to express the actual value of a corporation, as opposed to the current value based on the stock price. It is usually calculated by adding the current value of estimated future earnings to the book value.

junk bond
A high-yield bond that comes with a high risk of default. Junk bonds are generally low-rated bonds and are usually bought on speculation. Investors hope for the yield rather than the default. An investor with high risk-tolerance may choose to invest in junk bonds.

liability
An amount owed to creditors or others. Common personal liabilities include mortgage, car payments, student loans, and credit card debt.

liquidity

The ease with which an asset can be converted to cash at its present market value. High liquidity is associated with a high number of buyers and sellers trading investments at a high volume.

load

A sales charge or commission paid to a broker or other third-party when mutual funds are bought or sold. Front-end loads are incurred when an investor purchases the shares and back-end loads are incurred when investors sell the shares.

market capitalization

The current market price of a company's shares multiplied by the number of shares outstanding, commonly referred to as "market cap." Large-cap corporations generally have over $10 billion in market capitalization, mid-cap companies between $2 billion and $10 billion, and small-cap companies less than $2 billion. These capitalization figures may vary depending upon the index being used or the guidelines used by the portfolio manager.

market risk

The risk that investments will lose money based on the daily fluctuations of the overall market. Bond market risk results from fluctuations in prevailing interest rates. Stock market risk is influenced by a wide range of factors, such as the state of the economy, political news, and events of national importance. Though time is a stabilizing element in the markets, as returns tend to outweigh risks over long periods of time, market risk cannot be systematically diversified away.

market value

The value of an asset if it were to be immediately sold, or the current price of a security being sold on the market.

mutual fund

An investment that allows thousands of investors to pool their money to collectively invest in stocks, bonds, or other types of assets, depending on the objectives of the fund. Mutual funds are convenient, particularly for small investors, because they diversify an individual's portfolio among a large number of investments, more different securities than an individual could normally purchase on her own. Investors share in the profits of a mutual fund, and mutual fund shares can be sold back to the company on any business day at the net asset value price.

National Association of Securities Dealers Automated Quotation (NASDAQ)

A global automated computer system that provides up-to-the-minute information on approximately 5,500 over-the-counter stocks. Whereas on the New York Stock Exchange (NYSE) securities are bought and sold on the trading floor, securities on the NASDAQ are traded via computer.

net worth

The value of all of a person's assets (anything owned that has a monetary value) minus all of the person's liabilities (amounts owed to others).

New York Stock Exchange (NYSE)

The largest securities exchange in the United States, where securities are traded by brokers and dealers for customers on the trading floor at 11 Wall Street in New York City.

price-to-book ratio

Current market price of a stock divided by its book value, or net asset value. Sometimes used to assess companies with a high proportion of fixed assets or heavy equipment.

price-to-earnings (P/E) ratio

A measure of how much buyers are willing to pay for each dollar of a company's earnings, calculated by dividing the current share price by the stock's earnings per share. This ratio is a useful way of comparing the value of stocks and helps to indicate expectations for the company's growth in earnings, most useful when comparing companies within similar industries. The P/E ratio is sometimes also called the "multiple."

quotation

The current price of a security, be it either the highest bid price for that security or the lowest ask price. Sometimes also called a "quote."

real rate of return

The annual return on an investment after being adjusted for inflation and taxes.

reinvestment

The use of capital gains, interest, and dividends to buy more of the same investment. For example, the dividends received from stock shares may be reinvested by buying more shares of the same stock.

return on equity

The amount, expressed as a percentage, earned on a company's common stock investment for a given period. This tells common shareholders how effectively their money is being
employed.

risk tolerance

An investor's ability to tolerate fluctuations (including sharp downturns) in the value of an
investment in the expectation of receiving a higher return.

rollover

Immediate reinvestment of a distribution from a qualified retirement plan into an IRA or
another qualified plan in order to retain its tax-deferred status and avoid taxes and penalties
for early withdrawal.

Securities and Exchange Commission (SEC)

A federal government agency that was established to protect individual investors from fraud
and malpractice in the marketplace. The commission oversees and regulates the activities of
registered investment advisors, stock and bond markets, broker/dealers, and mutual funds.

security

Any investment purchased with the expectation of making a profit. Securities include total or
partial ownership of an asset, rights to ownership of an asset, and certificates of debt from an
institution. Examples of securities include stocks, bonds, certificates of deposit, and options.

socially responsible investing

Investing in companies that meet an ethical standard, by using a carefully employed screening
process before purchasing any securities.

split

When a corporation increases its number of shares outstanding. The total shareholders'
equity does not change; instead, the number of shares increases while the value of each share
decreases proportionally. For example, in a 2-for-1 split, a shareholder with 100 shares prior to
the split would now own 200 shares. The price of the shares, however, would be cut in half;
shares that cost $40 before the split would be worth $20 after the split.

Standard & Poor's (S&P) 500 Index

A market index of five hundred of the top-performing U.S. corporations. This index, a more comprehensive measure of the domestic market than the Dow Jones Industrial Average, indicates broad market changes.

stock

An ownership share in a corporation, entitling the investor to a pro rata share of the corporation's earnings and assets.

technical analysis

The use of charts and statistics to predict movements in securities prices. Technical analysis uses manual charts and computer programs to identify and project price trends in a market, security, mutual fund, or futures contract.

ticker

An information stream appearing on a movable tape or as a scrolling electronic display on a screen. The symbols and numbers shown on the ticker indicate the security being traded, the latest sale price of the security, and the volume of the most recent transaction.

top-down approach

An investment-selection method in which an investor first looks at trends in the general economy, then selects attractive industries and, finally, companies that should benefit from those trends.

total return

The change in value of an investment over a specific time period, typically expressed as a percentage. Total return calculations assume all earnings are reinvested in additional shares of the investment.

underwriter

A person (or company) who distributes securities as an intermediary between the issuer and the buyer of the securities. For example, an underwriter may be the agent selling insurance policies or the person distributing shares of a mutual fund to broker/dealers or investors. Generally, the underwriter agrees to purchase the remaining units of the security, such as remaining shares of stocks or bonds, from the issuer if the public does not buy all specified units. An underwriter may also be a company that backs the issue of a contract by agreeing to accept responsibility for fulfilling the contract in return for a premium.

value investing

An investment approach that focuses on companies that may be temporarily out of favor despite strong success potential or whose earnings or assets are not fully reflected in their stock prices. Value stocks will tend to have a lower price-to-earnings ratio than growth stocks, and are considered to be currently undervalued, making them good investment "deals."

volatility

An indicator of expected risk, categorized by the range of price movement of a security. It demonstrates the degree to which the market price of an asset, rate, or index fluctuates from its average. Volatility is calculated by finding the standard deviation from the mean, or average, return.

yield

The return, or earnings, on an investment. Yield refers to the interest earned on a bond, or the dividend earnings on an equity investment. Yield does not include capital gains.

Index

We Have EVERYTHING® on Anything!

The Everything® list spans a wide range of subjects, with more than 500 titles covering 25 different categories:

Business	History	Reference
Careers	Home Improvement	Religion
Children's Storybooks	Everything Kids	Self-Help
Computers	Languages	Sports & Fitness
Cooking	Music	Travel
Crafts and Hobbies	New Age	Wedding
Education/Schools	Parenting	Writing
Games and Puzzles	Personal Finance	
Health	Pets	